RIKKI BROWN'S SCHOOLDAYS

By Rikki Brown

LANG SYNE PUBLISHERS LTD.
GLASGOW

Published in 1996 by Lang Syne Publishers Ltd, Clydeway Centre,
45 Finnieston Street, Glasgow G3 8JU.

I.S.B.N. 185 217 024 7

Origination by Newtext Composition Ltd, Glasgow
Printed by Dave Barr Print, Glasgow

JUNGLE DRUMS.

Dedication – ALEX AND NANCY - SORRY ABOUT THE SWEARING.

THE sixties was a strange time in the evolutionary scale of things, the dream of the scheme was quickly becoming a nightmare of dampness and vile depression of the spirit.

The inner city had solved its immediate housing problems by shunting whole streets of people outwards, and ever outwards to the supposed Utopias. Easterhouse, Drumchapel and Castlemilk were to be the new Shangri La's but in actual fact the planners had demolished old Ghettos and created new ones.

It was simply new bricks with the same old tricks.

Inadequate leisure facilities caused spent enthusiasm, this wrought boredom, boredom bred vandalism, and vandalism led to the birth of a new renaissance of graffiti and violence on a scale unsurpassed since the Gorbals razor gangs of the Thirties.

The United Nations were called upon to send a peace keeping force into Easterhouse, but they were too frightened so they sent Frankie Vaughn.

The inhabitants at that time looked upon themselves as Frontiersmen and women and formed the ice cream vans into circles to fend off wild attacks from whatever 'Mad Mental' tribe ruled that week.

It was of course only the minority with big sticks who caused the undeserved ugly reputation but the jokes and the jibes abounded.

"Hey look at that dug, it's got two ears, must be a tourist."

I grew up in this atmosphere. I watched enthralled as gang fights ensued, yes enthralled.This was entertainment. It was long before the days of the video recorder and computers. It was the days when a video game was chucking a telly out of a window trying to hit a police car.

I looked upon this period of my life as my halycion days, my formative years or even my salad afternoons, and I based my future aspirations and career on my observations of this period in Glasgow's history.

I have no qualms about admitting where my childhood was spent.

The people of the schemes are pure Glaswegiana, perhaps these areas are not on any tourist walk or have any recommended must see scenic views but they are as much Glasgow as George Square and the City Chambers.

As with any city the inhabitants are the city and the Glaswegians traditional friendliness and ability to laugh at themselves has been well noted by the many visitors to Glasgow.

We have a character all our own and I am just glad that I am part of it.

Real names have not been used. All identities, including teachers, have been altered for obvious reasons!

1

CHAPTER ONE

PERHAPS this is an overly strong phrase but I did feel totally abandoned on my first day of school when I was delivered into the hands of an inane smiling maniac.

A crowd of mothers had gathered at the gates, some were in tears as they watched their offspring disappear for the first time ever from their sight.

Primary school is the pre big school where we go to formulate our early opinions of the world but all I recall from those early years is a story concerning the whereabouts of Chicken Licken and Turkey Lurkey.

One of the two had a nasty bump on his head and the whole plot centred on where he had recieved his injury.

What was to be learned from this literary masterpeice still defeats me. Perhaps it was subliminal.

We carried our school books in haversacks, usually army surplus canvas gas mask holders. We were the generation of the post war dream, the new elite, children of democracy and the new Europe.

God help the European Union.

I suppose in retrospect I did learn a lot from these years, how to deny convincingly that I was the recipient of a new haircut,how to tell a father's income by the sliding scale on the price of a dinner ticket, and to avoid sitting beside anyone with nits.

The Nit Nurse was a demon in the advanced stages of sexual frustration who would visit the school on a regular basis as a front line soldier in the never ending war against head lice.

She would grab your head and scramble through your hair like a mummy baboon looking for evidence.

If you were found guilty, she would adopt her disgusted face and spray some highly toxic product made from nuclear waste on your scalp.

We of course never knew the actual medical terms for any such conditions of the head. We simply called it the Meegy.

Poor families had the Meegy, the tell tale signs of poverty were there for all to see. The bowl cut was one, another was the scabby lips covered in glowing purple Gentian Violet. They would've been as well been carrying a bell and a sign which said Leper on it.

Children are cruel and have no respect for the feelings of such poor souls, they would be taunted regularly with shouts of, "Your house smells of cabbage".

This was long before air fresheners appeared on the market. In this age of memorabilia and nostalgia perhaps spray cabbage cans should be available to remind us of our roots.

Life then was an endless whirl of egg and spoon races and snotters.

The teachers didn't speak to us much, in fact the only time I remember being spoken to directly was when I was asked if I had a hankie.

I attended a Protestant school and we had a Catholic school opposite.

I was jealous of the Catholic kids as they seemed never to attend school much thanks to the celebration of certain Saints.

Religion was beyond me. I thought that it was to do with football.

Rangers fans went to Proddie school and Celtic fans went to Catholic school and Partick Thistle fans were athiests and didn't go to school at all but were taught at home by their parents.

At four o'clock most days both factions would gather opposite each other on a hill to shout abuse and throw clods of grass.

They'd shout *"Proddie dogs eat the frogs"* and our return volley was , *"Kafflick rats eat the cats"*.

It never got any nastier than that.

We'd see the Catholic kids being taken to the Chapel in what we assumed were wedding outfits. The wee boys in wee suits and the wee girls in wee wedding dresses. We didn't know it was their Confirmation, we just thought that Catholics married very very young.

When I was ten we were moved to a new annexe, actually more of an experiment than it was a school. We were to mix with Catholics, not in the lessons but in the playground.

Men in suits would come and watch us to take notes on our involvement at play with each other. We were Guinea pigs of the educational system.

As an experiment I suppose it was very low key and unsuccessful.

The lack of success was partly down to the Deputy Headmaster who was extremely wee free, fire and brimstone. He beleived that different religions should be segregated at all times and made his opinions well and truly felt.

After a few months the experiment was over and I was sent to Easthall School, the newest in Easterhouse.

I actually took things in at this school. Perhaps I was at the age of realising that I'd better. Up to that point when asked what I wanted to be when I grew up I would have no hesitation in answering *Bin Man*.

Why? Well for a start they got to ride on the back of the bin lorries and I likened that to being a rear gunner on a Lancaster Bomber,yes an exciting life.

My bombsights were aimed higher after the influence of my teacher at the time, a Mr McDonald. Although we were the children of a working class background he preached the betterment of one's social standing, he gave us inspired speeches on great Scots who had risen from the depths and lowlife areas to become Doctors, Soldiers, Politicians and Inventors.

I don't think he meant lowlife though in the same way it is meant today, well I hope he didn't anyway.

Name me one famous binman he would say.

Well there was one, Rakey Russell, the epitome of his profession, the ultimate midgie man. Rakey was so called because of his ability to find riches in the rubbish, he was the street corner hero and a legend.

Rakey would share soup from his flask with us on cold winter mornings and for that he was well liked.

His house was like the yard in Steptoe,everything he found had a use and he could fix almost anything. A broken chair,a burst couch,he even found a use for old 78's by moulding them into plant pots for his garden. He was totally self sufficient. What other people discarded he treated as though it was the treasures of the Incas.

He was quite well off and had a car. That was a sign of affluence to us. It was a Ford Anglia paid for by the money he'd made on the woollens he collected while on his route.

All we got from the Ragman was balloons. Rakey got money. He was smart.

Mr McDonald organised field trips to the country to educate us.

Showing us a tree or a flower, he assumed we'd never seen one. Although he meant well he was pretty condescending too.

He foresaw the European unity and decided that we should all learn French. He requisitioned a television from the powers that be and we were shown a programme on the Educational Channel covering basic French.

There was a problem though with the presenter, an unfortunately named Madame Anne Slack. Her name was enough to arouse sniggers, but her sidekicks were a couple of puppets whose names reduced the class to gales of laughter. They were called Clicko and Patapoof.

Everytime she said the name Patapoof howls of derision filled the classroom. This resulted in Mr McDonald charging around the class banging his belt on the desks but a nuclear deterrent would have been needed to halt the hilarity.

Madame Slack would say *"Now mes enfants repeat after me ,Je m'apelle."*

This was met with a chorus of *"FUCK OFF"*.

The whole class was belted for that one, Eddie 'the Beast' Beattie, perhaps the loudest kid in the class received a double dose for suggesting also that Madame Anne Slack should show the class her tits.

The Beast apart from being loud could also spit about twenty feet through a gap in his front teeth. This raised him to celebrity status as such talents were considered important.

The belt was very prevalent in those days and was used for every minor infringement of school rules. The belt worked, getting lines did not strike the same fear or have the same ring of glory.

"How many did ye get."

"Nane, I got lines".

"Ya fucking poof".

It was a very macho society in Easterhouse, at the age of eleven hanging around with girls was a cissy thing to do. Anyone caught doing so was branded and occasionally got their head kicked in too just for good measure.

We all fancied the girls but no one in their right mind would admit it. Affection was shown by stealing their skipping ropes or giving them a thumping.

The girls never understood our pre pubescent chest beating and the recipient of our 'adoration' would go and get her screaming banshee of a Mother who would inform us of her intention to *"tan oor arses fur us"*.

The mothers would all have curlers in and wear a headscarf over them to keep them in place. I thought this was some strange metamorphis brought on by severe aggravation, a bit along the lines of a dog raising its hackles when angered.

Close relatives were always used in threats.

"I'm getting ma mammie to you".

or

"Ma Da's bigger than your Da".

and on one occassion I heard,

"Hey you, my brother's no' all there by the way".

What this actually meant was probably a statement on their kin's state of mind but it did pay to read between the lines.

Then again half the class had some sort of mental deficiency. One loony was nicknamed Maddie, and according to many was from a different solar system, never mind planet.

He was called Maddie as he had all the self control of a rabid Alsatian who was already in a bad mood when the Vet diagnosed his ailment.

James Dean played chicken in Rebel Without A Cause, but we played a much more dangerous game called 'Maddie baiting'.

He was the size of a Gorilla, had the mind of a slug and would take these really scary brainstorms at the slightest provocation.

Maddie baiting became a sort in initiation into our gang. The rules were simple. You had to stand and repeat over and over loudly that Maddie was 'it' in a game of tig. That was it, that's all, no more, no less though this game saw more underpants changes than all the beltings the school had to offer.

Maddie took being 'it' as some imaginary slight and his brain patterns such as they were would mean that Maddie would come lumbering into action to try and kill the name caller.

He would chase his victim to the ends of the Earth, through walls, under oceans, through international time zones with the single purpose in mind of relieving himself of being 'it'.

My mate Dobbie and I were hanging about the back court one day when Maddie grunted past. We were a bit bored and decided to wind Maddie up to pass the time. We started chanting *Maddies it, Maddies it,* over and over.

He stopped and looked over at us. Obviously he had heard this noise and it was taking time to get into his ears and along the nerves into his brain. Once he twigged he trundled into action and came towards us with a menacing look on his face. We read the signals and got off our marks. He chased us from the back court, through the park, across playing fields, over hills and dales and across farm land in the general direction of Russia.

All the time the solid thump thump thump of his feet seemed to be keeping time with our beating hearts.

The pursuit had been going on for about half an hour, our legs were turning to jelly but we daren't stop to face the wrath of the devil beast.

Eventually we reached a high metal railing, I had nothing left to give and collapsed on the wrong side of it. Dobbie lept over it in a single bound and kept running until he was a speck on the horizon, so much for friendship and camraderie.

I lay there petrified and unable to move. Maddie stood over me. He blotted out the sky. He raised his hand. I closed my eyes and waited for the inevitable hiding. But he just tigged me and walked off.

I looked around for my guardian angel. Why was I spared? Oh thank you God, thank you.

Dobbie was eventually stricken by conscience and came back to prepare me for burial. I didn't tell him the true story of course, there seemed much more mileage in raising my social standing by putting it about that I, single handedly saw Maddie off.

It became a bit of school folklore and I went down in history as a man not to be trifled with.

Nobody would have believed the truth anyway.

My primary education finished very much the same way it had started, in confusion and fear. We were to be abandoned once again to stumble through the last stage of the scholastic process.

I did however have one long summer left before getting down to the real deal, the actual point of my existence which of course was trying to get some sort of educational qualifications which hopefully would see me progress to being a wage earning worker.

Secondary school was a daunting prospect as we'd heard all the horror stories of initiation ceremonies inflicted on the low life first year pupils.

Was Flashman alive and well in the East End of Glasgow, would we have our nuts roasted over an open fire. Would we fall victim to whatever fag system the bullies were operating and most of all would I survive the first day with my person and dignity intact.

CHAPTER TWO

WE spent the whole summer planning our campaign for what we called D.Day, the D stood for Doing. We had many long hours of discussion on survival and came to the conclusion that he who runs away lives to run another day.

We being The Beast, Doddie, Jacko and myself.

The Beast was probably the most philosophical and would often say,

"If they do us, they do us, there's no point in worrying about it".

That was fair enough but his plan was to spit on anyone who came anywhere near him, not exactly classy or hygienic but he reckoned that everyone hates getting groggered on. He even claimed that he was going to spend the summer smoking, that way he'll be able to do those sticky green ones that his smoker father does first thing in the morning.

I didn't fancy his plan much and neither did Doddie and Jacko. We favoured dogging it the first day and then wandering in the next after the beatings and kickings had died down.

I often wondered where this ritual came from.

"First day is it, sorry but we'll have to knock the shit out of you, school tradition you see".

Probably originated in public schools, but was altered from having to be rodgered by a peer of the realm's son in their world to getting a hiding from some ned in fourth year in ours.

D.Day arrived, our plan to dog it was discarded because it may have made us the centre of attraction and we wanted to remain as unnoticed as possible.

We approached the school gates, it was like High Noon, minus three hours of course. We were all wearing our school ties with very loose knots in a cocky men of the world kind of a way hoping that our sartorial white flag would be seen by the reception commitee as maverick spirit. Waste of time as it went unnoticed.

There were about 40 hardened pupils waiting, mostly third years with a few second years gathered on the fringes to sadistically watch a re-enactment of what they'd suffered 365 days ago.

The Beast turned to us and said in a commanding voice "just do what I do". Jacko piped up, *"what, we've tae shit ourselves tae then"*.

The Beast looked at him with distaste and said, *"look ya wanker, it's under control"*.

They gathered round us. We formed a square standing back to back.

The boots and the fists came flying. I don't think there was much malicious intent involved but I don't suppose that was the point.

We were saved by The Beast who pulled an air pistol out of his schoolbag and yelled *'right ya bastards, fuck off'*. He was waving it about and informing everyone that it was loaded with a dart.

They all backed down except one of the third year pupils who was shouting something about his lot ruling the roost and first years can't be allowed to get away with this sort of behaviour.

The Beast shot him in the thigh and he started to cry.

All his mates started to laugh at him and this made him cry even more.

The bell rang and that was it, we were in. We trooped off to the main door followed by shouted predictions on the longevity of our lives.

Our secondary education had started. The first day was fascinating. I had never seen so many girls with breasts.

The curriculum was explained to us, we were to have different teachers for every subject. We were given schedules, French, Biology, Chemistry, Geography and so on. Our first lesson saw us seperated from the girls in the class, they were off for Domestic Science and we were off to Technical Drawing.

After about ten minutes wandering the corridors we found the room called hell and stoking the furnace was Beelzebub himself, or to give him his earthly name Mr McCrindle.

He hated us, it was obvious though I found out later that he hated everyone.

To us he seemed about seven foot tall, he probably wasn't, more of about six foot eleven. He towered over us explaining the rules of engagement.

Speak out of turn, the belt, scratch your name on the rubber, the belt, deface your jotter, the belt,late for class, the belt, farting noisily, the belt. I'm sure he said breathing , the belt but maybe I'm just exaggerating for comic effect.

The rules were etched on my brain in 30 seconds flat but for some it was too late. We had been issued with jotters, on the covers there was a warning on road safety which stated *"Danger Danger Danger - better a moment at the kerb than a month in hospital"*.

In registration class the first thing that The Beast and Jacko did was to write an R over the D in danger and add an S at the end.

Their jotters now showed allegiance to Ibrox.

RANGERS, RANGERS, RANGERS.

McCrindle walked round the class checking out our kit like some martinet sergeant major. He picked The Beast and Jacko from the ranks and paraded them in front of the class.

Explanations were useless. He produced this belt from under his jacket. The belt could stand upright and must have come from an animal with a very very thick hide.

He gave The Beast and Jacko two strokes each, the sting echoed around the room and the windows seemed to vibrate. We could see their hands redden and feel their pain. He beckoned them to return to their seats.

Rikki Brown's Schooldays

We had been in the school for half an hour and already two out of the four of us had suffered the ultimate punishment.

The Beast sat down next to me and whispered *"big bastard, I'll get even wae him"*.

He did...... eventually.

After that double period came playtime and we gathered in the playground to discuss events. We were joined by another couple of pupils who had come from another primary school, Winker and Jim.

Winker told us that his big brother had been to the school a few years before and had warned him about Mc Crindle.

"Aye my brother says, he enjoys belting people cos it gies him a big stiffie".

We'd had a pretty miserable start, 50% hit rate, we reached a 100% a few minutes later. Teachers were positioned at the windows to watch for trouble and they didn't have to wait long.

As we were standing talking a wasp kept buzzing about our heads. I was shooing it away but as you know wasps are persistent wee bastards.

I got fed up with it and swung my hand round to clobber it in mid air, missed it and my fist connected with Doddie's jaw.

He was stunned, I was stunned, the wasp stuck up two fingers and kept buzzing us, next thing Doddie and me were rolling around on the deck exchanging blows with chants of *"oh oh oh" ringing in our ears*.

We were dragged apart by Mr Menzies our registration teacher. He hauled us back into his classroom and gave us three of the belt each.

Our wrists were marked and from then on so were we.

The Jungle Drums had begun to beat, the word was out and the unruly element had been indentified. From that point on we had no chance in any class. They were waiting for us.

Everytime we entered a classroom our names were called out and we were ordered to occupy the front seats. Within two days Winker and Jim's names joined ours in the register of bad boys after they were caught writing rude words on the English class blackboard.

After a month though we had the situation sussed. We knew which teachers we could wind up and which ones would beat you to within an inch of your life for some minor infringement.

As the weeks wore on we settled in. We picked the girls we wanted to sit next to and impress with our bravado and derring do.

We thought we were the characters, probably the whole school thought we were just wee tubes with big ideas, but at thirteen you are not exactly sensitive to public opinion.

By November we had all been selected for the school team, the four of us already played for a local team called Lochbridge so we moved as one unit. In actual fact it would be nearer the point to say that we all just chased the ball. This was in the days before team tactics and we played in a sort of a one - ten formation, that is to say one goalie and ten centre forwards because everyone wanted to score.

If you scored it was glory, if you didn't you were a diddy. Nowadays every shot at goal is applauded with "*oh hardlines and good try*" but in the appreciation of effort times it didn't matter if you had passed the whole defence, rode some scything tackles, made the best shot in the world but missed, you were called some very hurtful names.

Our P.E. teacher and team manager was Mr Watson, we never liked him much and he disliked us. The only reason he managed the team was for the overtime, in fact his whole management function was to hand us the strips before the game then count them as we handed them back in.

We had a not bad team but it is very hard to control a mouldmaster football on cold winter ground. It would have been easier to catch a bullet between your teeth than stop this ball on the bounce.

The mouldmaster was solid and dimpled. After every winter game we'd go home with mouldmaster marks on our thighs and our foreheads, the result being that we looked like victims of some strange skin disease.

Bad enough in itself, but playing on red ash pitches led to you losing half the skin off your leg if you were brave enough to slide tackle anyone.

Our first tough game was against St Leonards, a catholic school not far from our own. This was our old firm, 11 prods against 11 kaffliks.

We had quite a crowd, even a lot of the teachers had turned up hoping to watch us getting our come uppance once and for all. They didn't have to wait long.

The Beast and Jacko were sent off for kicking players off the ball and we were down to nine men but we rallied round. A cross came over from Jim, I went up and next thing I knew I landed on the top of my head on the solid ground. I had been hit hard on the thigh and spun upside down.

I couldn't get up. A teacher ran on and asked me how many fingers he was holding up. I failed the question and he diagnosed that I had concussion. I was taken off and driven home in the school mini bus.

Jim who was another blue nose now also had a body to match as he had been kicked up and down the park. We lost three nil, and had suffered a humiliating defeat at the hands of our rivals, but as luck would have it someone had sneaked into their dressing room and thrown all their clothes into the showers and turned them on. So on the whole the day didn't end too badly.

CHAPTER THREE

SCIENCE was a favourite subject in our circle. We all had visions of becoming great scientists and learning how to blow things up with the maximum devastating effect.

Our aspirations had been noted by the powers that be and in first year we were only let loose with a piece of litmus paper, a magnesium strip and a low power bunsen burner. Hardly the things nuclear weapons are made of.

Still we did have fun with the Chemistry teacher Mr McLean who bore an amazing resemblance to the Gestapo officer in the T.V. programme Hogans Heroes. We called him Nutty because of his quick temper and the speed at which he could run down the class foaming at the mouth to haul out a miscreant.

He would start a minor experiment, nothing in the least dangerous and we would let bangers off at the crucial moment. He would jump, drop his test tubes and then belt the whole class.

Ours was always a tiring period for him. He even belted the females who in our gentlemanly manner we would usher to the back of the line.

By the time Nutty reached them he would be exhausted and the effects of the belt would be much lessened.

During one lesson he was showing us this glass tube which he called a pipette, the class dreamer Shuggie McMillan, a lanky kid with faraway eyes was staring out of the window lost in a world of his own.

Nutty was most offended at Shuggie's lack of interest.

He threw a piece of chalk at him *"Boy!!!, what is this glass tube called?"*

Shuggie sealed his and our fate.

"A durrette sir, naw that's a rubber johnie bag int it, I dunno".

Nutty flipped and belted the whole class whilst screaming that we were all damned. Shuggie took his punishment and went back to staring out of the window as if nothing out of the ordinary had taken place.

Perhaps he thought that corporal punishment was normal in working class schools, the system roughening up our hands for the manual labour we would aspire to when we left without any qualifications.

Xmas was fast approaching and the corridors were littered with crepe paper decorations and really bad paintings of Santa drawn and water coloured by the year's equivalent of remedial class - 1F.

1F comprised real no hopers and they were only issued with one jotter and a packet of crayons, pencils being considered too sharp and dangerous for them. They would be taken on field trips into the country and abandoned, but like stray pets they always found their way back to the school, much to the disappointment of the student teachers who had been landed with them.

We had a school play, my lot being an A class were given speaking parts,the F class always played trees or bits of scenery. I remember one of the trees took stage fright and pished all over the highly polished wood, this resulted in us skidding all over the place on our big entrance.

Another feature of the end of term was the school dance. All through December we would be dragged screaming and kicking down to the games hall to learn the niceties of Ballroom and Scottish dancing.

We had to learn the lot, from the St Bernard waltz right up to the Gay Gordons of course this was in the days before Gordon came out of the closet.

The lessons were a total shambles, Watson the P.E. teacher would line up the boys on one side of the hall and the girls on the other.He would then stick a crackly 45 on the school Dansette record player and order us to choose a partner.

No one budged from the pack of macho 13 year olds. Dancing was for poofs, but out came the belt and threats were issued with increasing venom until we complied and shuffled across the floor to pick the girl we least fancied. We would never have actually picked anyone we did fancy, that just wouldn't have been right.

There was never enough boys to go round and about half a dozen girls ended up dancing with each other.

None of us made any attempt to be graceful and just walked up and down the floor holding our partners as far away as possible.

Everytime Watson's back was turned we'd make hand signalled lewd suggestions to each other showing what we would really like to do to the girls.

The lessons proved useless, even if anyone could dance no one would have admitted it for fear of ridicule.

The night of the dance arrived and the six of us turned up late thinking this was the cool thing to do. We were all really shiny and stinking of Old Spice. We had shared a can of lager and assumed therefore that we must all be pished.

The dance was in full swing, well as full as it was going to get anyway. Three or four couples were sharing the dance floor and Mr Menzies our registration and history teacher was walking amongst them and separating anyone who was going in for a winch.

After about half an hour of abject boredom and making eyes at the talent who on the whole were studiously ignoring us the music stopped.

On came the Headmaster Mr Clark and gave us the same speech we were to hear from him at every school dance.

"Boys and girls,or should I say little ladies and little gentlemen you are all looking splendid tonight, a credit to your parents, indeed yes.Now we have had the traditional music and as a special treat we are now going to hear a couple of beat numbers from the Westwood school group The Conspiracy, but before that I'd like you to give a big hand to Mr Menzies and Miss Campbell who have given their

time here to chaperone the events, hip hooray, hip hooray".
All he got was two handclaps, both coming from the teachers.

Given their time, that was a joke, the minute the dance was over they'd be in the back of his Triumph Herald doing Biology homework.

That was the only reason they'd volunteered.

We all thought this but in actual fact were all a bit jealous as it was generally agreed that Miss Campbell was the school babe.

The school group came on, a sorry bunch of 4th year terminal acne cases, and subjected us to murderous renditions of the latest chart numbers.

They began with Slade's Coz I Luv You and ended with Deep Purple's Black Night. During Black Night the guitarist had a brain storm and thought he was playing the Apollo. He went into this supremely fucking awful five minute guitar solo punctuated regularly with off key notes.

The set finished and the silence was deafening, the band stood there waiting for applause. It didn't come.

The Beast who was something of an authority on music captured the moment best when he said loudly, *"what an absolute load of shite".*

I wish I could report a romantic end to my first school dance but there was none. The Beast got off with a caution for his outburst.

Seemed that Menzies agreed with him.

We approached the end of our first term with gleeful anticipation. We had survived our first term at the big school and we looked forward to starting the second as seasoned campaigners.

Before the break up of term we had one more task to perform. We had to look interested at the school's en masse trip to the local church for the Xmas service.

The teachers looked upon this as the last battle of wits of the term.

From the first year to the sixth year there were about 1000 pupils and the teachers had to supervise the half mile walk to the church, all the time keeping a watchful eye for escapees.

They lined us up in the playground and we set off in a four in a row line stretching about 400 yards.The teachers had positioned themselves at intervals of 20 yards for the forced march.

To onlookers we must have looked like prisoners of war being escorted to a Stalag in Nazi Germany.

Some of us didn't fancy the prospect of sitting in a church for two hours so we had laid our plans to abscond well in advance.

We weren't alone. Every year had its escape committee and the older pupils were very well versed in the art of escaping.

We decided that we'd wait for someone else to break away and in the confusion we'd sneak away.

We'd gone about 100 yards when two third years darted up a close, our guard

Menzies spotted them and unwisely gave chase. We saw our chance and ran up another close and onto the first landing.

We looked out of the window and watched the line snake away round a corner.

We had made it. We waited five minutes to make sure the close was clear and walked out into the street, straight into the Headie who was bringing up the rear. Apparently this was what he did every year, being firsties we didn't know that and our names ended up in his January Book. His January book was full of the names of the pupils he was going to belt on the first day on the new term.

So much for a coded postcard from the freedom of Switzerland.

CHAPTER FOUR

WE spent the whole two weeks of the holiday playing football. We always played football. There was a bit of spare ground behind our row of houses which doubled as Hampden. As the area was derelict we didn't have to use our imagination much.

No matter how few or how many people turned up we could play something resembling a game of football.

If there were only two we could play 'Cannie'. This involved standing two empty lager cans up and trying to knock them over. Three of us and we could play 'Three and In", one in goals and the other two versus each other, the object of the game was to score three goals and then take a shot in between the jerseys.

As being in goals was never too popular, only very half hearted attempts at saves were made.I think Scottish goalkeepers must have played a lot of Three and In.

When we had enough for teams we'd play various matches depending on how long we had. If there was loads of time we'd play a ten/twentyoner with ten being half time and at the other end of the scale it would be a five/elevener.

It also depended on the weather or our boredom threshold.

If we had uneven numbers one team was allowed a backsie, backsies are goalies who can play outfield too. Generally speaking it was always the worst player in the team who ended up in that confusing position.

The games were often violent, especially if we were playing an opposing street or gang. As there was no referee no one was ever sent off and bad tackles were always settled in a square go after the match.

We preferred playing football in the winter. In the summer the nights were endless and every apres tea time game was joined by men home from their work. We didn't have any choice,they'd come on and use their wieght and height to attain the glories they didn't have the talent for in a game with their peers.

In the winter the games ended before these Peles and Gertie Mullers got home from work.

The girls never appeared in the winter,they were always at home swapping scraps. I never understood why they had Charles Dickens books filled with wee bits of coloured paper with various sized cherubs on them. We swopped blows, they swopped scraps, it was only later that we'd learn the workings of the gentler mind.

Looking back I suppose the mania for collecting did span the sexual barriers, while the girlies were collecting scraps we boys were amassing chewing gums cards such as the Man from Uncle set or American Civil war cards. The latter were horrific colour drawings of war at its most violent. Men impaled on wooden spikes after an unsuccessful attempt to rush a cannon, decapitated bodies lying on the battlefield.

At that tender age war was glamorous.

We loved all things pertaining to human destruction - Airfix kits comprising Spitfires and Hurricanes, Action Man dolls, Commando comics and toy guns.

We even played a game called 'Best Mans Falls". Someone would sit at the bottom of a hill and pretend to be the enemy.We'd shout down what weapon we'd like to be killed by, mortar, machine gun, bazooka etc.

The winner was the person who died in the most spectacular fashion. I was particularly good at death by hand grenade.

Nowadays you wouldn't really play that game as death by laser guided missile doesn't have the same ring to it, and anyway you couldn't do it convincingly unless you could shoot forty feet in the air and spread your internal organs over a very wide area.

We would also collect Bees in jam jars. We would poise ourselves over a lump of clover, open the lid deftly and capture some poor unsuspecting Bee minding its own busines.

As I recall, once captured the Bee had no chance.It was out and out cruelty, but we disguised it as curiosity.No torture was too obscene and we could have taught the sadistic Jap prison camp guards in the Commando comics a thing or two.

Strange as it may seem we had no stomach for cutting up frogs in the Biology class. We'd flinch while the girls started crying and accused the teacher of being sick. To this day I still have no idea what cutting up frogs would have taught us. It's not as if anyone left school and got a job as a frog doctor, yet frog dissection was right up there with Algebra.

Algebra was the unknown for my class, no one could understand it.

I remember the teacher, Mr Russell or Tranny as we called him because he had a hearing aid, explaining as best he could the workings of the subject.

He got a reaction much the same as if he was explaining $E = Mc$ squared to a class full of Orangutans fresh from the jungles of equatorial New Guinea.

Once after rabbiting on for half an hour on the principles Winker put his hand up and said, "*So fuck*".

Tranny looked at him and decided that any reaction was better than no reaction and said that we could apply algebra in later life when we had secured gainful employment. Winker's hand went up again.

"*What as sir, fuckin' astronauts*".

Tranny gave him the belt. This time Winker had over reacted.

Other subjects too seemed totally pointless like Physics for instance.

What was the reasoning of time in motion, a small wheeled object running down a slope attached to a tickertape to tell us its speed in comparison to its mass weight.

As Winker would have said "*So fuck*".

We returned for our second term most of us wearing awful Christmas present knitwear. We must have looked like a classroom full of juvenile Val Doonicans. Jim had the most ridiculous one, it was covered in reindeer. Every time someone looked at him he would say *"look it's freezing ootside, allright"*. On the first morning back the Headie's voice came on the intercom and summoned those in his January Book to present themselves in his office for a belting.

At least he had the decency to wait until we'd heated up because as anyone who has had the belt will tell you, the pain is ten times worse with frozen hands.

In February we were offered the chance to go away for a week to the school's camp in Millport. All we had to do to qualify was to get our parents to sign a wee form saying that in the event of us not returning in one peice the school couldn't be held responsible.

My parents signed mine with undue haste.

Millport was over the sea, well a wee bit anyway and we were all really excited. Twenty four of us were to go plus Mr Menzies and Miss Campbell. Roy Jones the language lab technician was going too. It was thought that the headmaster had sent him along to keep an eye on the teachers' fledgling relationship.

We set off in the school mini bus bright and early one Monday morning.

Roy was driving and we the bad boys were sitting at the back as far away as possible from the love birds who were occupying the front seats.

The girls occupied the rest of the front half of the bus.

We spent the first half of the journey giving the two fingers to any motorist who was unfortunate to be travelling behind us but eventually it became boring.

Everyone was in high spirits and inevitably the singing started. We, being the 'lads' refused to join in so the girls started singing.

'The back of the bus they cannae sing, they cannae sing, they cannae...'

They were interrupted by The Beast who stood up and shouted over their dulcet tones *"naw but we can fight like fuck"*.

Menzies was not a pleased man as he had hoped for a week of peace and quiet to continue with his wooing of Miss Campbell. He reckoned the outburst was a portent of things to come and realised he had gone away with the kids from hell.

He decided to try a new approach with us as he knew that threats and violence would not work, so he gave us his 'little adults' speech.

"Right that's enough, we are all grown up here and it's about time we acted like it. We have left the confines and the constraints of the school and we are going to have a pleasant week. We are going as friends, not as teachers and pupils, now you can call me Colin this week, Miss Campbell's name is Linda and you all know Roy, so let's be little adults".

Winker thought the prospect over for a minute or two.

"Colin".

"Yes Winker".

"Are you gonnie be spending the week trying to slip Linda the mitt".

We arrived at the place the school called Hush Hush, it had been a secret naval base during the war and the name had stuck.

As soon as the mini bus had stopped we went off to explore but that took us just about ten minutes as Millport, apart from being a lovely wee scenic place, really has nothing else but a bit of scenery.

The whole place seemed to be full of rabbits running around banging into things. We returned to base and asked Roy the question , *"Hey how come all the rabbits over here are pure pished"*.

Roy told us *"that they weren't pished"* , they were suffering from Myxomatosis, a disease given to them by man to stop them breeding and overrunning the island. The Beast suggested that maybe Colin should be given a dose of it to control his amorous intentions.

Roy laughed, he had a sense of humour, either that or he was just humoring us. Roy was about 20 and had just qualified and if it was the former I'll put it down to the fact that he hadn't as yet acheived the distance of the pupil and employee of the education department relationship.

Our first night in Hush Hush was spent in the sleepless pursuit of trying to get into the girls' dorm. What we would have done once we'd managed to sneak in was a mystery but we felt it was traditional to try.

Sex at this point was something we made snide jokes about but didn't have a clue as to the whys and wherefores of the act. We did know that it involved a man and a woman, so at least we had a grasp of the basics.

At breakfast the next day Colin gave us the entertainment schedule. Day one we were to go into the town and hire bicycles which we would then use to ride round the island, wooo - such excitement.

I asked him why we just couldn't go round the island in the mini bus which prompted a dirty look and a lecture about fresh air in the lungs.

Roy was given the task of driving us into town as Colin and Linda were staying behind to prepare the evening meal.

Roy dropped us off and disappeared into the pub. He gave us two hours to do our tour and said he would then meet us back at the hire shop.

We got on our bikes and headed back in the direction we had just come. It was about five miles back to Hush Hush and we called the rally the *'let's catch them with their knickers round their ankles cycle race'*.

We cycled back like demons, cackling like maniacs as we went. We got back and they were indeed preparing the evening meal. Colin was sitting outside peeling potatoes. He did however have a glow of smug satisfaction about him so we did wonder. He also knew what we were up to as we could see it written all over his face.

With nothing left to do but cycle round the island that's what we did.

There is a rock there with a crocodile's face painted on it, no doubt with a grant from the National Trust, perhaps they were hoping it would become the 8th wonder of the world. It didn't.

We goaded Colin the best we could for the first couple of days and he took it in suprisingly good humour. It was only later we found out that he was just biding his time. As in H.G. Wells War of the Worlds - slowly and surely he laid his plans against us.

On the third night he appeared at the hut door carrying a fishing net and a torch. He then made a great play of acting casually. We feigned disinterest until he selected a log and began to bang it off the floor.

Satisfied with his choice he went outside and we followed him out as curiosity had now got the better of us.

"Colin, what's the gear for".

He told us that he was going to hunt Bull Rabbits for the next day's dinner, hunting, now this was more like it. But what was a Bull Rabbit and how are they caught. Colin explained.

"They are male rabbits about twice the size as normal and they were nocturnal, they could easily be identified by their large antlers".

The way to catch them is to run along the road stretching the net across it, the Bull rabbit will be stunned by the torchlight and you then crack them over the skull with the log."

Being from the city and not too well versed in the flora and fauna of our native country we believed him and the prospect of satisfying our schoolboy bloodlust was far too much for us.

We asked if we could have a go. He handed us the equipment and sat on the entrance gate and watched us charge off down the road.

There were about ten of us running along the dark roads and screaming our heads off. Winker was following with the torch and Doddie was behind him with the log. Every so often a car would come along driven by a local. They'd slow down to look at the bizarre scene of ten smiling loonies armed with a net, a torch and a log.

Once they had decided that we must be mad they would speed off screeching rubber.

We must have run for a couple of miles before we decided that the Bull Rabbits were in bed and dejectedly we made our way back to Hush Hush.

On the way back the torch batteries ran out and every so often one of us would yell an oath as we fell into a ditch.

We reached Hush Hush to find the place strangely silent and in total darkness. We approached cautiously and edged our way through the door.

All the lights went on and Colin was standing with all the females who were screaming and laughing. We'd been had, well and truly had.

Colin was beyond smug as he had made us look like total idiots in the eyes of the girlies, not only that but he'd probably raised his self esteem with his 'burd'.

We retired for the night sheepish and quiet, but we would have our day and we slept soundly with that knowledge.

Waking early the next morning we convened a war cabinet behind the main hut and decided that the situation called for a clever scheme with something to throw him into a blind panic.

Winker came up with a plan.

We made a dummy out of clothes and stuffed it with grass and straw, for an added touched of reality we used a turnip for its head with Winker's Rangers tammy on it as the final touch.

From a distance it looked quite lifelike. We took it out to the shoreline amongst the rocks and put it in the water. After letting it drift out about ten yards The Beast ran into the hut screaming that Winker had fallen in, banged his head and was now in the advanced stages of drowning.

Colin came running out, quickly surveyed the situation and waded in to rescue the dummy. He actually looked quite heroic.

It was only on reaching the dummy he realised he'd been duped and we all started cheering. He waded back, got out, dripped his way past us and back off into the hut to dry off. We'd had our revenge and decided to call it quits.

On our last night anyone who wanted was allowed to go into the town unaccompanied. Only four of us took up the offer, the rest wanted to stay and sing songs round the campfire that Colin was building.

Roy drove us in and disappeared off into the pub.

The Beast, Winker, Doddie and myself found this cafe and went in for some soft drinks. A few of the local kids sat about and every so often threw us a dirty look.

Not that this bothered us at first as we were from Easterhouse and thought we were dead tough, but eventually it became annoying and The Beast asked them *"what do you think you are looking at ya pricks"*

He elongated the word prick adding a bit of venom into it for scary effect.

One of the locals said "nothing" and The Beast said "well ye'd fucking better not be".

There were only three of them and we were four, not bad odds in the event of things turning nasty. We soon got bored with the cafe and walked outside and up towards the pier. The locals came out and followed us. Winker looked back and said *" what's their problem".*

It wasn't their problem it was ours. All along the walk they were joined by more locals coming out of houses and by the time we got to the pier there were about twenty of them.

Once on the pier we were trapped, there was only one way out and that was through them.

"What now?" said Doddie.

The Beast was in no mood to back down.

"What are youse wankers wanting?"

They didn't answer.

"Are yeez fucking deaf?"

They just stood there staring at us.

Winker took a couple of steps towards them and they stepped back.

"They're fucking shitebags, mon then, come intae us".

He held up both hands and was beckoning them with his fingertips to come forward.

The biggest one spoke.

"We're the Millport Young Team"

"Wooooooo" said The Beast, *"the Millport Young Team. Well yeez urnae going to live long enough to be the Millport Old Team, so come on, are we going right ahead or whit".*

The Beast whispered to us *"act mental and they'll shit themselves".*

We started shouting names at them and generally looking as though we weren't right in the heads.

I am ashamed to say it felt good. Four against twenty and they were looking very aprehensive and stood there not knowing what to do.

Obviously they couldn't back down and by this stage neiher could we.

The deadlock was broken when the only cop on the island turned up in his Panda car and they scattered.

We stood our ground.

"Right, what's going on here".

"It was them, they followed us".

"I assume you lot are from Hush Hush".

"Aye".

"Is there anyone with you".

"The language lab guy, he's in the pub".

"Wait here and I'll go and get him".

Roy was pissed off at being dragged out of the pub and drove us back in silence. We told him it wasn't our fault but he just ignored us after saying, *"yeh right".*

We got back to Hush Hush and found everyone sitting round a huge bonfire singing campfire type songs. Boring !!!!!, especially after our night out.

The next morning we piled into the mini bus and headed homeward.

When Roy started up the engine there was a cheer, only Colin and Linda looked unhappy at the prospect of returning to normality.

That summer in Easterhouse violence reached an all time high, or an all time low, depending on which way you looked at it.

Gangs appeared everywhere and every four hundred square yards of area was laid claim to by teams of loonies with varying scars and I.Q's.

The Pak, the West Rebels, the Torran Toi, the Skinheads and the Bar-L ruled their individual turfs with open razors and sharpened steel combs.

None of my crowd were allied to any such organisation as we deemed it far too dangerous. We liked to move about and if you were in a gang stepping two feet into the wrong area would see the invader of territory getting "chibbed".

We all lived in Skinhead Land, tales of the heroics of its members became part of folklore. For some reason a lot of people idolised these guys but I always found them to be psychotically deranged.

One night a gang fight started and we sat on a gable end watching the proceedings, one gang would shout abuse then charge, they'd run so far then stop whereby the other gang would stop, shout abuse and chase them back the way. This was generally the scenario but on this occassion they must have become confused and met in the middle.

In the ensuing slaughter Doc Martins, razors and various other weapons were being used to maximum effect. This was better than the telly.

The fight was between the Skinheads and the Pak, the Skinheads thanks to numerical superiority gained the upper hand and the punishment laid upon the Pak was fierce.

One guy was being held down while a stiletto knife was being thrust up his anus and the knifeman was shouting *"aye let's see the fucking doctors stitch that"*. Another victim was being held with his legs apart and a Skinhead was swinging a golf club and trying to knock his chukkies onto the green. Yet another was being sat on and his head was being knocked from one side to the other by a Skinhead with a half brick in each hand.

It was total carnage, the next day on a wall next to the battlefield someone had spray painted: Skinheads 9 Pak 0.

The police always took their time in turning up at gang fights. They'd start their sirens from about six miles away giving everyone plenty of warning that they were coming.

I figured their angle was that if they left these fights long enough the gangs would probably kill each other off and save them a lot of paperwork.

We had other diversions in the summer, the Wimbledon fortnight.

Most of the year we played football and then for no apparent reason we would take up tennis for two weeks.

We were all crap at it but none the less we'd troop down in droves to the council tennis courts to emulate the tennis stars of the day.

We couldn't afford rackets but for 3d you could have one on a hire/steal basis. We used this plan, at the end of the game you would hit the ball out of the court and casually go to get it. The parkie would be watching and when you got to the ball you started running away with the racket. While he was giving chase the rest of us would run out of the court and disappear off in different directions.

There really wasn't a lot of point in this though because every council racket had property of Glasgow Corporation Parks Department stamped on it. The only courts in that area were the ones from where the rackets got nicked, so you really couldn't go back there and use the racket or you'd get done for theft.

Occasionally we would try other pursuits. If someone turned up with an old wooden shafted golf club we would all have a shot at hitting the ball until we lost it.

Rounders too was popular. Rounders is a bit like baseball and it was the only game we'd let the girls participate in because we always beat them.

During one game we were approached by a couple of Mormon missionaries, but instead of giving us the usual lecture on religion they asked if they could join in. They took off their jackets,one delivered the ball to the other, he swung the racket baseball style and the ball shot off in the direction of Edinburgh. We never found it and it would have taken us two bus journeys just to go and look for it.

He was very apologetic and promised to replace the lost ball. He was a man of his word and the next day he turned up with a brand new tennis ball in a wee brown paper bag.

We felt sorry for the Mormons. They believed in some strange religion which worshipped blue and brown suits and short hair. They were also so far away from Salt Lake City, their homes and probably everything they deemed normal to be thrust into the East End of Glasgow to have doors slammed in their faces or asked if they knew the Osmonds.

The funny thing was though, Mormons could walk unmolested through any part of the scheme. I think they were looked on as part of the scenery like trees, sparrows or stray dogs.

I don't think they actually converted anyone as they would have had more chance of turning water into wine than a Protestant or a Catholic into a Mormon.

CHAPTER FIVE

THE summer drew to a close and we started hanging around the barbers shop watching for the next intake of pupils being made ready for their first term at the big school.

When they came out with their new haircuts we'd tell them in graphic detail about the tortures they were going to endure on their first day.

We told them that there was this guy in fourth year who would pull off their arms and hit them with the gooey end, in fact he was famous for it. This got a few of them scared but most just looked at us as though we were stupid.

The day arrived and we gathered like vultures at the school gate, the toughies we had encountered on our first day were there.

The first one arrived, his bag was opened, his playpeice was taken out and stood upon, then he was given a few swift kicks up the backside and told to be on his way.

We were standing sniggering at them and calling them names and shouting watch out for the Mad Arm Pullerofferer. As saying that was quite difficult I think it only came out right once.

We also were there to check out the female intake for talent. It was common knowledge girls only fancied pupils of the year above as dating someone in your own year was considered uncool.

As we were now second years so we assumed every first year female would fancy us.

Puberty was kicking in and with it came an interest in the opposite sex but in the age of innocence we had all our facts totally wrong.

Sex education was a thing of the future and in those days we had to discover things for ourselves.

For instance we thought a Poof was a cow's joabie, because....when a cow did its business the result was something resembling a Pouffe chair. Made perfect sense to us.

It was when Winker wrote Franny McCafferty is a Poof in the mud during a football match and was given a kicking for it were we told what it actually meant.

We had this mate who was a couple of years older than us and he told us his brother had done 'it' with a girl.His brother had explained to him the process and now he was giving us it second hand.

He told us that a man puts his thing next to a woman's thing and they got this wee electric shock and that was it, dead simple.

One of the listeners took the whole thing quite literally and thought all that he was missing was the electricity.So he got his father's old car battery out of a cupboard and jump started himself with a set of jump leads. He ended up in hospital, his name said it all - Willie Burns.

We all jumped in with snippets of knowledge. Doddie had been leafing through his mother's catalogue, the bra section to be exact and discovered what breasts were for thanks to a picture featuring a front opening bra for breast feeding. That's not how he put it though, he told us that a woman's diddies served the same function as a cow's bagpipes.

A derogatory term we applied to everyone was Wanker. We didn't know what it meant but everytime we used it in the classroom we were given the belt.

Armed with or without this information we approached the second year as five foot lotharios ready for the challenge of helping a female reach the heights of carnal pleasure.

We waited a bloody long time.

We still had the same teachers and still the same lessons but they were at a slighter higher academic level. For some pupils this was to be their second last year at school and they decided that they'd better learn something. We were the last intake who could leave school at fifteen as the authorities had just changed the earliest leaving date to sixteen.

We settled down to our studies with a new vigour and for the first time we actually listened to what the teacher had to say. The teachers however viewed this with great suspicion.

Mr Brown our woodwork teacher was by far the most suspicious. He became so nervous of our intentions that he'd check that we hadn't sawn through a leg of his chair before he sat down.

About two weeks into the term he entered the class and found Winker with the class Ug's - Bugsy Millar's - head locked in the vice and thumping him with a piece of four by two. Winker had caught Bugsy looking at his willie in the shower after P.E. and took exception to it. Mr Brown belted Winker but the relief on the teacher's face was evident and it was obvious he was glad to see the class return to normal.

In English we started to do Shakespeare which was met with an attitude approaching hostility. All the thy's, thou's and ancient dialect was beyond our comprehension and we just recited it parrot fashion unsure of what exactly was coming out of our mouths.

Our English teacher was a woman in her mid thirties, Mrs Cairney, and she had this habit of sitting on her desk with her feet on the chair in front of her. From every angle you could see up her skirt. Winker and myself were always stuck in the front row and got more of a view than anyone else.

One day Winker turned to me and said, "*ye can almost taste it can't ye*".

Fortunately she never heard that comment but when she asked Winker to read something off the board and he replied "*maybe if ye moved yer fanny out of the way I could see the board*" it was plain for all to see that she'd heard that one.

Winker was stunned. He hadn't actually thought that his mouth would say what his brain was thinking, but it did. The class sat in shocked silence. Winker was dragged out of his seat and along to the headmaster's office where he was given 12 of the belt and suspended for two weeks.

When he was allowed to return to the class we were about to do Hamlet and Miss Cairney had a special treat in store for Winker.

He was given the part of Osric the Fop. She went on in great detail explaining exactly what a fop was. This only resulted in Winker dogging English for a further fortnight to avoid being labelled a jessie for the rest of his school life.

I was given the part and I suffered.

After two weeks Winker returned figuring he was now safe as the die had been cast. Wrong. He was given the part the moment he popped his head round the classroom door.

October saw the annual Glasgow Schools Athletic Challenge heats. This encompassed all the schools, from the schemes to the upper echelons of the posh areas.

Our heat was against Knightswood and technically speaking the posher schools did spend a bit more time teaching and training their pupils in field events. So it in reality was always a gubbing for the working class schools.

But we had the world's best athlete at our school and things were going to be different. His name was Johhny Tucker and he had been nicknamed 'Run Like Fucker". He had it all, good looks, he was smart and he could pull the birds. In American terms he was the school Jock.

Johnny was two years older than me and he had done 'it'. In my book he should have retired right there and then, how could he ever surpass glory like that? But he did.

On the day he won the 100 metres, 200 metres, the 100 and 200 metre hurdles and led his year to a 4 x 100 metres relay win.

The girls loved it and the guys in the school gave him a grudging admiration, even though we called him a big poof behind his back. Anyone who could beat us at anything in our book was a big poof.

I was picked for the 400 metres, my training for the event seemed to be endless running round the track in a string vest, baggy black cotton football shorts and a pair of half crown sand shoes.

I was informed that my times weren't too bad and I at least stood a chance of coming in fifth. Fifth because there were four runners from my school and four from Knightswood,they would all beat me but I'd beat my lot.

When my turn came I purposely strode onto the track, a little man with big job to do.

The Knightswood mob were kitted out in all the real gear, real running vests, shorts and spikes. We looked like we were sponsored by Oxfam and they didn't.

The gun went off and the race commenced: at the 200 metres mark I was in the lead, as much a surprise to my feet as it was to my heart which was thumping away like the big bass drum in the Orange Walk.

With a 100 metres left to go I was still leading but tiring, everyone was egging me on except my mates who were making 'wanker' signs at me as I passed them. 50 metres left, 25, 10 and I hit the tape before anyone else. I staggered a further few metres on and collapsed in a heap.

I had beaten the spikes. Winker ran over and told me that all through the race you could see my chukkies hanging down below the shorts. This was a little more information than I really needed to know.

He also added that I was a 'daft bastard' because I'd knackered myself for the 4 x 100 metre relay.

I didn't care. I just lay there the hero basking in my glory. If Tucker could get a bird by running, now surely should I.

News of the victory spread through the school and I was a bit of a celebrity for a week until I had a really bad game in the football team and we got beat seven nil. After that things returned to normal.

The drudgery of lessons continued unabated. It was long periods of boredom punctuated by short bursts of anarchy. The teachers went through the motions and so did we.

It was now 1971 and things were in a transformation. Fashion became ridiculous. We already had flares but only hippies and pop stars wore them. Now we had something much much worse, baggie trousers. They were 30 inches wide at the thigh and 30 inches wide at the bottom. The comic look was worsened by a 9 inch waistband. The really fashion conscious glitteratti had theirs made to measure by a tailor in Glasgow city centre called Arthur Black. Anyone with enough cash could be made into a clown.

Our school uniform had changed from Gloverall Dufflecoats and a pair of Levi Stay pressed into Gloverall Dufflecoats and 30 inch bags and the Headmaster put his foot down. He gathered us all together in the hall and lectured us on the ettiquette of the school uniform. Up until this point he had been quite liberal but now he had decided enough was enough. Anyone appearing in the school in 'Bags' would be sent home.

The next day there were a lot of clowns wandering the streets very aimlessly.

Music played a large part in our lives and how we dressed. Slade fans for instance wore Doc Martins, denim jackets and sported skinhead haircuts while Heavy Rock fans wore Doc Martins, denim jackets and sported long hair. Note once again the subtle difference.

Everyone seemed to wander around with an L.P. under one arm. An album in those days when it came to rock comprised an A side containing one track of guitar and drums solos and a B side of exactly the same.

I recall one night gathering in Shuggie the dreamer's back room to suffer 23 minutes of Jimi Hendrix's Voodoo Chile. Every ten seconds Shuggie would excitedly point out an oncoming guitar solo and try to play along with it on a poxy Spanish guitar with nylon strings that his mother had got him for his Xmas.

Hendrix fans were a breed apart from the rest of us. They were the people who would scrape off the insides of the banana peel and smoke it saying *"what a high man"*. I did try it but it never worked for me. I was told I didn't have the right vibes for a hit.

New words started appearing in our language, *far out, heavieee, and stoned*. In Easterhouse it caused a lot of confusion, if one were to say *"I'm gonnie get stoned the night"* it either meant that one would be partaking of a banana roll up or had the intention of walking down the wrong street and criticising the local gangleader.

Being in a group became the cool thing to do. All the girls were into pop stars and 99% of them had I Love Marc Bolan written on their schoolbooks and school bags. With that in mind we decided to start a band with the idea of strumming our way into their underwear.

We had our first meeting in a guy called Kenny's house. Kenny was a year younger than us but he had a big brother in a band and the equipment was stashed in his house. We knew this, befriended him and asked him to join us.

At our first meeting we discussed the stuff we would play and who would play what. Kenny said he would be the lead guitarist, The Beast on drums, Jacko on rhythm, Winker on vocals and me on Bass.

We visited the Congregational Church 50 yards along the road from Kenny's house and asked the minister if we could rehearse in the hall.

Being a kindly soul he agreed as long we we didn't break or steal anything. We carted all the stuff along and set it up.

"Right" said Kenny *"we'll start with Free's Allright Now"*.

Kenny hit the first few chords while the rest of just looked at each other. Kenny stopped playing, *"what do you not know it then?"*

"Aye we know it but we don't fucking know how to play it".

Kenny looked at us.

Winker piped up, "I *know the words*".

The Beast added, "So what, we all know the words".

Kenny said "Okay it's the chords C.F. and G, then the rest is simple."

Jacko asked him, "So what's a chord then"

Kenny put his guitar down *"Can any of you lot actually play anything?"* He directed the question to Jacko and myself.

"Well naw, no really".

Kenny had a look of puzzlement on his face. *"Well how the fuck can we start a band then?"*

The Beast hit a drum a few times. *"Well this bits' a fucking dawdle"*.

Winker said *"knowing the words must be a start as well"*.

Kenny went on to explain the principles and being able to play something was high up on the list. He added that he had been playing the guitar for three years and it was not an easy thing to play well. Then for good measure he informed us that the only way we could play together was for us to back him on a comb and some toilet paper.

After a lot of cajoling he agreed to teach us and within three weeks we had learned to play one number badly. Fame was just around the corner. We were just in the process of learning our second number when Kenny's big brother's band went on tour and took their equipment with them.

That was the end of that.

CHAPTER SIX

WHEN you are fourteen years old you start to think of yourself as a wee bit grown up, almost adult, things start to happen to your body, hair grows where it's never grown before and you have this strange and foreign stirring in your loins. I think it's called puberty.

We started to notice girls a lot more. In fact it became the most important thing in our lives. We became obsessed with the female form and the most perfect form in our school belonged to Linda Fraser, who bore a remarkable resemblance to one of Pan's People - those awful dancers on Top Of The Pops - and it was rumoured that half the boys in fourth year were crying themselves to sleep over her.

I sat next to Linda in Geography, I sat next to her in English, I sat next to her any chance I could get.

Winker noticed my interest and told me one day, *"You fancy Linda Fraser don't ye"*.

I was embarrassed.

"Naw I don't, I think she's a dog".

The rest of the lads were sniggering at me. *"How comes ye always sit beside her then, we're gonnie tell her that ye fancy her"*.

I could only deny my romantic interest but the bastards still told her or as they put it, *"I wanted to go with her"*.

I started finding love hearts with our names written on the school walls. Everytime Linda and I passed in the corridor I was pushed against her by one of my so called mates.It was all juvenile stuff but it was giving me a great big 'reddie'.

I started sitting next to a girl who was known as Souffe. Even If I'd spent 50 years in solitary confinement, was blind and stupid, no one could accuse me of fancying Souffe.

She had many problems, a wee tad on the smelly side, dandruff like a snowstorm, her plukes weren't so much plukes as they were enormous pus filled boils and things would jump out of her head which she would then kill by smacking with a ruler.

I started to scratch myself too but it was better than being ridiculed for the human failing of being fond of a girl.

After this episode Linda and I sort of drifted apart and she left school that summer. I didn't see her again until three years later when I was in fifth year.

I was stepping off the bus from Glasgow early one Saturday evening. Another bus had pulled in behind at the same stop and a figure disembarked. The figure looked familiar. I still recognised the shape but the mode of attire was to say the least a tad bohemian.

It couldn't be Linda, who always wore the latest fashions but it was her in a worn out woolly jersey, a a pair of ripped jeans and a stupid looking Sherlock Holmes type hat.

She approached me and said hello and asked me how I was. I was lost for words but I did manage to blurt out that I was glad to see her and how long it had been.

I was passing her house and we walked together. We went through the usual 'how is everyone' etc and as we got to her house she asked me what I was doing later on, and would I like to come to her house and listen to some records.

Would I! I tried to play it cool. *"Well em"* all this time my loins are going off like a greyhound after a hare, *"yes sure"*.

Alone in Linda Fraser's bedroom, life's ambition to date.

I ran home, had a bath, brushed my teeth away, put anti-perspirant on every part of my body and slung on half a gallon of my dad's Old Spice.

I was ready, a love god. I didn't set my sights too high. I promised myself that I would be content with a winch. No I wouldn't slip the mitt and make a fool of myself. I was going to play it cool!

I arrived at her door an uncool 45 minutes early and her mother let me in. She told me that Linda was in the bath.

Her mother was friendly and I felt at ease. She asked me if I would like a drink. I said no. She asked me if I was driving and I replied, *"no I'm walking"*. I think she thought I was being sarcastic but I wasn't.

After what seemed like an eternity Linda appeared. She looked great although she was wearing slightly strange hippy clothes.

I was invited through to her bedroom. It was so dark that I banged my knee on a cupboard and a pain shot up my leg but I put on my *'naw it wisnae sore at all face'*. She lit a candle and a couple of what looked like firework tapers. The smoke smelt of flowers. Apparently it was incense. She bade me to sit on the bed. I did so and reclined myself. Just as I was getting relaxed her mother came in. I shot bolt upright and banged ny head on the bookcase above her bed, books flew off, landed on the candle and the room plunged into darkness.

What was I saying about cool.

Her mother said she was going out and wished us a pleasant evening. Great, I had her alone. My boyhood dream was going to come true.

Linda got some matches and relit the candle and it made for quite a romantic scene. I started trying to smell my own breath to check of halitosis.

"What are you doing?"

"Em I've got a bit of fluff on my hand and I'm trying to blow it off".

She put on a record and it was the most mournful bloody thing I had ever heard. It was like a dirge, it droned on and on and on about being dead and depressed or depressed and dead, I can't remember which.

She lay down on the bed beside me and I thought this is it so I tensed my lips. I tensed and tensed and tensed, nothing.

All that was going through my head was when are we going to start the winching.

"*Can you feel it*" she asked.

"*I will if you want me too*".

She nudged me.

"*The music, can you feel the music*".

If truth be known I thought it was total crap but I played along as criticising her musical taste at this point would be strategically a bad move.

"*Yeh, it's great, who is it, I might get a copy myself,*" I said lying through my underpants.

"Leonard Cohen".

In the weeks to come I came to hate that name and I wished that he and all his family would die in some horrible accident. The more horrible the accident the better.

We lay there and she played Leonard Cohen all night. Each song was worse than the other. He sang about death and suicide, the bastard was driving me to it.

My eyes were stinging with the incense, my lips had cramp from pursing them and I just couldn't find the right time to make my move.

After we had been through every album the fucker had ever made she put the bedroom light on and handed me a book.

"*This changed my life*".

I looked at the title. Beautiful Losers by yes, you've guessed it Leonard bloody Cohen. She went on to explain that she used to get drunk and have indiscriminate sex, basically she had fallen by the wayside and her life had no aims, but after reading this book she had changed her ways and her life now had direction.

The basis of the book was that everything in the universe has a brain, a heart, feelings and a personality.

In short it was total hippy bollocks. Linda would now have intimate conversations with inanimate objects and she did. She told me that her rubber plant was her best friend and he knew everything about her.

I thought that she really should get out more.

Linda started quoting passages which she had underlined. I had listened to his music all night and that was enough, winch or no winch it was time to go so I made my excuses.

She said she would walk me home, now there was a novelty and one up for feminism.

All the way along the road she would stop and talk to the trees, the grass and lumps of fresh dog joabies. It was embarrassing and at one point I was leaning against a fence waiting for her whilst she told this tree that she loved it when a couple of drunk men passed.

"What's up wae yer burd pa?"
"Aye is she on the waccy baccy?"
I replied that it was her hobby.
They walked on but one of them turned back and, said *"I used to collect stamps but I didnae fucking feel the need tae talk to them"*.
He did have a point.
Eventually after conversing with all the flora in Easterhouse we reached my close, she pecked me on the cheek and wandered off into the night. I did feel a tad guilty about letting her walk home herself but after the night I had just had I thought to hell with it.
We started to see each other quite regularly and she still kept going on about Leonard Cohen and her new found appreciation of her dignity and self respect, me being a devious wee bastard and more than a bit desperate I was waiting for her to have a relapse and I'd be In Like Flynn.
One night she asked me if I still kept in touch with the old gang. I did keep in touch with most of them but she was in actual fact refering to her old school boyfriend Andy.
"I wouldn't mind seeing him again, just for old times sake".
I would never have classed myself as a pal of Andy, I always thought he was a bit weird but I did know him and I didn't see anything wrong at the time in visiting him with his old girlfriend on my arm.
So one Saturday night we trooped up to his house. He was glad to see us and led us into his bedroom. It too was dark and smelt of incense but I didn't put much emphasis on it at the time.
After school he too had found a hobby. He was now into Black Magic and Black Sabbath. We had all dabbled in the usual mince like saying the Lord's prayer backwards into a mirror while eating an apple and contacting the spirits via the medium of the ouija board, but Andy had gone far beyond the realms of teenage curiousity.
He produced a table top from under his bed. On it were painted pentangle and strange letters but what caught my eye was a large bloodstain in the middle of it.
He explained casually that he had been sacrificing cats to appease the devil.
Why Lucifer actually needed appeasing was not explained but it was nice to listen to someone else make an arse of themself for a change.
Linda set herself the task of reforming Andy back into the normal happy weirdo he was at school. She would explain the error of his ways and his trip into Dennis Wheatleyism (her words, not mine).
They would argue about God, the Devil, cats and Leonard bloody Cohen.
Andy mentioned that he was very appreciative of what Leonard was trying to achieve through his work.
I thought Leonard, on first name fucking terms are we.

It was then I knew my days were numbered.

Linda started visiting him on her own in her crusade. About a fortnight later I visited him and found that he had painted "*I LOVE LINDA*" with emulsion on his bedroom wallpaper.

I was gubbed, still they made a nice couple and would often visit the park together, her talking to trees and him no doubt nailing cats to them. I retired gracefully but one lasting effect of that episode is that I still really really hate Leonard bloody Cohen.

As we approached the end of second year a heatwave struck. It's funny but when I look back I can never remember it raining much. I'm sure it wasn't but if it did I can't actually recall it.

The classrooms were stifling, the windows acted as a magnifying glass and we squirmed about in our seats hot and sticky. We were in the Physics class on a boring double period. Our teacher was a man we'd given the name Shazzan to because he had a wee goatee beard and looked like a character in the programme the Banana Splits.

Shazzan should never have chosen teaching as a profession as he was far too highly strung and nervous for it.

Whether it was the heat or the fact he'd been teaching people who wouldn't listen to him all year I don't know but it was during this double period that the end of his tether was reached. In fact it audibly snapped.

He had asked the class a question and everyone was shouting out answers.

"A million sir".

"A cabbage".

"Forty five and a quarter degrees Sir".

"Tuesday".

He shouted above the melee "*right who said forty five and quarter degrees*".

Thinking that it was the right answer and although I hadn't said it I was going to take the credit for it. I stuck my hand up.

"*Me Sir*".

He flipped and dragged me out of my seat, out into the corridor and began to belt me with a vengeance.

I protested my innocence, I was the one who shouted out cabbage and surely that was a stupider answer than the one I was being punished for. He continued to belt me. Mr Smart, an English teacher in the adjacent classroom heard the smacks and assumed he must be belting the whole class and came out to give him a hand.

When Mr Smart saw that only one pupil was on the recieving end he ran along and grabbed the belt from the by now frothing Shazzan.

"*For gods sake man what has he done?*"

Smart must have thought that I'd assassinated the whole class to merit this.

Shazzan was shouting, "*he said forty five and quarter degrees*".

He was still trying to get at me and Smart had to hold him back.

Shazzan had lost it completely. I thought so, as did Mr Smart.

I was ordered back into the classroom and told to wait there while Smart took Shazzan off to see the headie.

I opened the classroom door and all those who had been behind it scurried back to their seats. A cheer went up.

Shuggie said I had been given 23 strokes but Winker said it had been 25. Winker was the smartest so I beleived him. If Winker was right I'd set a new school record.

On the downside though ugly weals were starting to appear from my wrists right up to my elbows. I was checking them when a relief teacher entered the class and told me to report to the Headmaster.

I wandered off fully expecting another thumping.

I knocked on the door and a smiling headmaster opened it and bade me to sit down. He then told me that he regretted the incident and asked me if I would be taking the matter further. I wondered what he meant.

Obviously he assumed that I would tell my parents and they in turn would kick up a stink in the education department.

Actually he was very straight with me. He said that my punishment far exceeded what the department deemed reasonable, then he got to the point. Would I be charging Shazzan with assault?

We had been goading Shazzan all year and as far as I was concerned the ice we had been walking on with him was thin to say the least.

I informed him that I had no intention of telling my parents, mostly because they would have been of the opinion that I probably deserved it.No the furthest this would go would be into the school record books and we would leave it at that.

He looked relieved,thanked me and I returned to the classroom via the toilets where I ran my wrists under the cold water tap to try and take the pain away.

Back in my seat Winker told me that Shazzan had been given the rest of the year off as he was suffering from stress. I didn't bloody wonder.

CHAPTER SEVEN

THE third year at school was the year of division,those who were leaving, namely Dobbie, Jacko and The Beast formed a different pack and would while away the days either dogging it or smoking behind the games hall.They decided that they were now adult and would soon be going out into the world to make their way, the rest of us were still kids with in some cases three years still to go.

I was staying on as I wanted qualifications in the hope of avoiding a manual job. I had seen the workmen building the new school extension in mid winter and thought bugger that. Men blue with cold with their breaths turning to frost as they swore when their hands were too numb to get their thermos flasks open for some hot soup.

No I wanted a cushy job. In fact my only ambition was to make the most amount of money for the least amount of work, but then again isn't that everyone's.

Only Winker and myself were staying on in our crowd, nearly three quarters intended leaving as soon as they legally could. It was quite sad really as a lot of them had brains but the call of the overall in the Wills cigarette factory was just too strong.

We gained new additions to our crowd. Big Ally Dixon, a tall blond kid's who wouldn't have looked out of place in the Hitler Youth. He was also a very brash and abrasive character who had knowledge far beyond his years. The other was Wilco, a studious kid with glasses who was famed for his one liners and his impersonations of the teachers.

The four of us became the school pupils committee for our year whereby we were allowed to take teachers to task over any grievances real or imaginary we may have.

One of the major moans was the school never took us on trips anymore.

Not since Hush Hush had we engaged in any extra curricular activities, so after a lot of argy bargy it was decided that a trip to the theatre wouldn't bankrupt the school funds.

Unfortunately the trip coincided with our curiosity with alcohol and we decided to visit a pub before we went on down to the Theatre.

We arranged to meet in the Stevedore and Taylors pub at the top of Buchanan street (sadly no longer there, they should have put up a plaque saying 99% of under ages had their first drink on this site).

I arrived first in my new three piece suit looking as much an 18 year old as a 15 year old can possibly be.To my astonishment the barman asked me what I wanted and not being to well versed in the arts of ordering a drink I asked for a drink of Guinness.

"What dae ye mean a drink, pint or half pint".

"A pint".

I got my PINT and sat down, it tasted vile,the only reason I had asked for Guinness was because I'd heard the comedian Dave Allen talking about it on T.V.

I sat there with it feeling very ill at ease but trying to look as though I had been in pubs all my life.

The other three came in, Big Ally went up to the bar and ordered, he was also served and brought the drinks over.

He looked at my pint tumbler.

I replied it was guinness.

"That's a fucking Tims drink".

He took a sip from his own glass containing lager and went off to the toilet.

We sat and surveyed the surroundings, the place was full of wee jimmys with gruff woodbine voices and they spoke in some strange dialect we couldn't understand.I later found out that this is the common langauge of those in the advanced stages of alcohol abuse.

Big Ally returned and said he'd been in this pub a hundred times before and he was a regular. We sat in awe as he criticised the staff, the decor and the fruit machine which he refered to as a "Fucking rip off".

He went up to the bar and returned with a brandy and a cigar, sat back down looking a bit like a gangster in an old black and white movie.

"Good brandy this, yeh brandy is my tipple".

He took a drink and then a large puff on his cigar, it looked really cool until he choked and spat his drink all over Winker and Wilcos faces.

"Aw fur fucks sake".

The whole bar turned round to look at us and there we were, four fifteen year olds, two looking embarrassed and the other two looking wet.

We drank up and left.

We met the rest of the class down at the Citz, we had two teachers supervising us and they gave us the rules, stay together, stay out of the bar and stay out of trouble.

Ally said that the teachers could go fuck themselves and asked me if I was coming to the bar for a drink at half time.

I think it's called the interval in the theatre I told him.

"Well are you coming to the bar in the fucking interval then".

We'll see.

But after watching a very bad play about the Americanisation of Japan in which the lead character said "Gee Dolores" all the time I was ready for any diversion at the interval.

"Mon, we'll hide in the corner, no one will see us".

We only had enough money left for one brandy, so there we were, Ally with his brandy smoking a cigarette and Wilco and Winker outside looking in through the glass panels.

Ally must have had a very weak bladder because he asked to me to hold his drink and his fag as he was going off for a "desperately needed pish" as he put it.

Stupidly I took his accoutrements and was standing with them when the teacher walked in.

He saw me and came straight over.

"What the bloody hell do you think you are doing?"

I started to stutter but denials were usless as I had the evidence in my hand. Ally cane back in, clocked the scene and got off his mark.

I reported to the teacher next day and got six of the belt.

A month after this I had my first real drink.

It was someone's 16th birthday party in Blairtumock House a large mansion in the public park. It was the only thing remaining from the family who had once owned the land Easterhouse was built on before they sold up and moved on.

It was now hired out for functions and we were all invited to attend on the Saturday night.

Big Ally said he would arrange the bevy so pre party we went up to his house for a wee swally. When he said he would arrange the swally we thought he meant can of lager, but no, his father worked in a whisky bond and periodically he would drain the sediment from the bottom of the vats and take it home with him.

It tasted vile but diluted with cream soda it was very palatable indeed. At that age you have no concept whatsoever of the effects of alcohol and there we were knocking back pints of the stuff.

At first we felt great, absolutely great, the world was ours and everyone was our friend.

We left the house and staggered the 400 yards or so to the party and made our big entrance. We had arrived and no bother to us by the way.

I spied the school captain sitting next to a girl. I shuffled over and in my alcoholic inhibition said to him. "I think you're a fucking wee prick".

Statement made I then collapsed on the floor and started, for the want of a better phrase, puking my load.

I dragged myself off to the toilet and just lay there with my head down the pan. One by one Ally, Winker and Wilco appeared and did the same thing.

We lay there for three hours unable to move. I asked God many times to let me die but he obviously wasn't listening. We were all wretching violently and anyone who entered the toilets could see our backsides in a formation puking team sort of a thing.

We couldn't move and lay there semi comatose. We were getting a lot of verbal abuse for hogging the toilets and at one point someone came into my cubicle and pissed over my head. ·

I like to think he was aiming for the pan but in retrospect he probably did mean to hit me as I was probably pissing him off.

The party ended at 10 o' clock and we had to leave but couldn't stand unaided. We were gathered up by those more sober than we and taken along to another party. I had an my arms over two guys shoulders and my feet were getting dragged along behind me.

On the way there I lost a shoe.

We reached the other venue and it was a smarty party, ie - no drink and just sweeties. I was past caring anyway.

I was hauled into the living room and deposited in front of the T.V. and collapsed in a heap much to the annoyance of the host's Father who was trying to watch Scotsport.

I couldn't even sit up for appearances sake, I just lay there limp and with one shoe missing.

Eventually we came round enough to walk to Ally's house, albeit with the aid of fences, parked cars and each other.

We went into his bedroom and collapsed and lay there fully clothed covered in and stinking of vomit.

Winker managed the strength to say, "See as soon as I feel better Dixon I'm gonnie kick your fuckin' head in ya bastard".

Ally didn't answer him as he was too ill.

Thankfully I ended up in the arms of morpheus and I awoke next morning very surprised as I was sure I would have passed away in my sleep.

One by one the other three awoke. Winker claiming that he was blind in one eye, Wilco with a translucent face and Ally none the worse for wear.

It was at this point that we decided we hated him.

After a lot of moaning and groaning we decided to head home to recuperate and the three of us started what seemed like an endless trek homeward. The sun was splitting the trees and the light was boring into our eyes like a black and decker drill.

I was hobbling as I had lost one shoe but was far too ill to care. We split up and went up our own streets.

I passed my mother who was on her way to church with her friends, she looked at me, declined to comment and kept on walking.

I got home and slid into bed. It felt great to get under the covers but no sooner had my head hit the pillow than my father started to hoover the house and stick a Sydney Devine record on the Dansette.

At that point I reached the lowest ebb in my life. Incidentally it was another four years before I touched a drink, even the smell of lager was enough to bring the sorry scene back and make me vomit.

CHAPTER EIGHT

WE returned to school on the Monday still feeling god awful but we were cheered by the news that the school had been given a grant to buy musical instruments.The money was intended for Cellos and Flutes and the likes but after a Teacher/Pupil discussion we persuaded them to release the funds for guitars and drums. After our first musical foray, which ended abruptly, we were going to get another chance.

The whole school wanted to be pop stars and have access to the equipment but after a lot of threatening behaviour from Winker and Ally we got exclusive third year access. The fourth year boys started a band also and we rehearsed on alternative days.

We had slightly more knowledge than they did though and they soon got bored with it and left us with total access.

To justify the expenditure we would have to play the school dance, the Headie came up with a list of songs he thought it would be nice if we could learn.Winker took one look at the list, saw Beautiful Sunday, and ripped it up.

We remembered the fiasco of the first school band's appearance and decided that we would have to be much much better than them. We wanted people cheering and shouting how great we were, not how shite we were.

The equipment was top of the range, at least if we weren't exactly brilliant we would sound good.We now had a different line up: Winker on vocals, Ally on drums, Kenny on lead guitar, me on bass and this bloke Ronnie that no one liked except Kenny. Since Kenny was the best amongst us and we needed him we had to go along with his Ronnie decision.

We rehearsed most days and became quite proficient, the only problem we encountered apart from Winker's ego was volume.

We'd start off balanced and you could hear every instrument clearly then someone would decide that their guitar was too low and turn it up. This led to someone else turning theirs up and so on. Pretty soon all you could hear would be Winker screaming above the feedback.

We needed a name. For some reason Winker decided that he was the band and we were his backing group and thought the name Winkers Blue's Warriors was quite apt. No one agreed with him.

"Oh aye fuckin' popeye, why stop there, why not Winker and his Wankers?"

It was settled democratically when Ronnie beat Winker up and we simply became the Blues Warriors.

We were to play for the first year's to kick off the dance season, and as the night of the gig approached our confidence ebbed and we started crapping ourselves.

We sat backstage and listened to the usual "heelan' records come to a close and the Headie giving his usual speech.

He said will you now welcome the Westwood School group, the ...the...

he went into his pocket for the piece of paper with our name on it and eventually got it right.

The curtain went back. Before we took the stage Ronnie went off to the toilet and we'd forgotten to tell him we'd decided to open with Alex Harvey's Midnight Moses instead of Deep Purple's Strange Kind Of Woman.

The result was chaos. He was playing one thing and we were all playing another. For some reason he blamed Winker for this and called him a stupid fucker.

We composed ourselves and started again. This time we were all in tune with one another and suprised ourselves so much that we all had broad grins on our faces, which was hardly the mean moody look we were going for but we couldn't help ourselves as we were on a roll.

After a few numbers the crowd actually started to dance and at the end of a song went into wild applause.

We finished the set and left the stage.

They were screaming for an encore, we went back out but as we had exhausted our full repertoire we had to repeat a couple of the songs. They didn't care.

We finished and walked off after Ally had walked to the front of the stage and threw his drumsticks into the melee and they started fighting over them.

This was glory, this was fame and we went backstage and started congratulating ourselves until Ronnie who was strangely silent throughout all the backslapping said, "well whit did ye expect, anything's better than they fuckin' ballroom records, that lot would have asked for an encore if I had farted".

He was always capable of putting a dampener on things.

Ally was well pissed off with him and a few weeks later murdered his budgie 'Tottie' in a revenge attack.

After the Christmas break we returned to school for what was going to be most of the class's last term. Those of us staying did our best to learn but the leavers had no intention of spending their last five months in any sort of educational pursuits and the classes were disrupted at every opportunity.

One by one the leavers played truant then disappeared entirely.

This left the rest of us to ponder the advantages of a long term education. Fifteen is an awkward age, money or lack of it had become important and in a few months time our classmates were going to become wage earners whilst the supposedly brainier lot wouldn't see any real cash for another three years.

It was a tough choice to stay or leave but my parents had attended one of the parent's nights and were told that I had a chance, so from then on I had no choice. I was staying on for the duration and that was that. I said I could leave after the O' levels and get a job then but no, I was ordered by Gruppenfuhrer Dad to get

Highers as well.

The lessons at times seemed inane and pointless but I felt I had to learn something for my parents' sake.We were not a rich family and as they were going to have to fund me for a further three years I'd have to give them some gold at the end of their rainbow.

It was a strange changeover. Once the teachers had learned that we were willing to listen a bit their attitudes altered. We still had a mischievous streak but they were now more apt to view our 'getting through the day' with more humour than we thought was possible.

Our Geography teacher was a Mr Johnstone and he looked every inch like a Geography teacher. He had glasses, cords, tweed jacket and thick walking shoes. Come to think of it he looked more like a Vet.

His classes were fun. If we asked stupid questions we got stupid answers.

He had a way of handling the class that we'd never come across before. If we didn't want to learn we were to sit at the back of the class and amuse ourselves and if we did want to learn we were to sit at the front and listen.

Also on entering his class Winker and and myself were ordered out to the front.

"Any jokes, comments or remarks before we start".

"Em...no Sir".

"Great, now sit down".

It worked and we very seldom misbehaved. His classes were interesting probably because he didn't teach us normal geography and would basically just tell us of his travels and strange encounters he had experienced. We loved it and I'm sure he had a soft spot for us.

He was also the only teacher who caught me red handed and never belted me. One Friday afternoon he left the room to go to the toilet and while he was away I was hit on the back of the head with a rubber by Crammond, a really irksome kid who had one of those faces you just want to slap.

I jumped out of my seat, grabbed Crammond's bag and swung it above my head. I had started the swing when Johnstone walked back in and it was too late to stop. Crammond seeing the teacher enter thought he was safe and clasped his hands on the desk in innocence instead of protecting himself. The bag almost dislocated his head from his shoulders.

Johnstone asked us to the front of the class.

"It's Friday and there's only five minutes to go before you and I commence our weekend, now I have caught you assaulting another pupil, maybe Mr Crammond deserved it, I don't know so I am going to flip a coin, heads I belt you tails I don't".

He then flicked up a ten pence and I guessed heads:

"Very lucky, return to your seat".

I could have sworn I saw a tail.

Our attitudes changed towards all our subjects. In English Mr Smart was looking for volunteers for the end of term play which this year was to be Macbeth and all the kids who had been so much trouble the year before now offered their services. He accepted with a humble show of gratitude that we actually found quite embarrassing.

I ended up playing MacDuff and Ally was to have the starring role of Macbeth. The school plays were always a culmination of the year's work in English and a chance for the teachers to show the attending hierarchy from the school board what they had achieved.

The day arrived and everyone had worked really hard. We had costumes, make up and scenery. This was to be no Am-dram production, we knew our lines and we were pros.

The matinee was for the pupils and the evening performance was for the parents so we were expecting the evening slot to be met with more appreciation.

The first scene involving the witches was met with jeers and cat calls.

"Hey look there's yer burd" etc.

It was to be expected. What wasn't expected was Ally's ad libbing. He walked onto the stage in tights, make up, cape and crown and someone in the audience shouted, "Ya big poof".

Ally forgetting the first rule of theatre - the show must go on – replied with great wit and professionalism,

"Right which one of you bastards said that?"

Mr Smart, in the wings, was whispering loudly to him to get on with it.

"But one of they bastards called me a poof".

The school board members who were sitting in the front row were tut tutting and making notes.

Smart by this time was in a panic so he brought the curtain down and ran over to Ally and gave him a short sharp lecture on the principles of theatre. He reminded him who was watching plus a hint at how miserable he could make his life if he didn't get on with it in true thespian style.

Ally looked at me, "Right you watch who shouts out and we'll knock fuck out of them the morra".'

The curtain went up and my head was popped discretely round the side of the stage, but this time also teachers were dotted about the hall ready to haul any would be theatre critics out for a hiding.

The play this time went without any major mishaps and Mr Smart was congratulated by the board members. He had survived the test of his teaching skills.

The evening performance was even better and no one accused Ally of being a big poof, he went home that night with the success of his first big thespian adventure coursing through his veins.

About a week later I saw him running after the school magazine editor with a copy of the magazine clutched firmly in his grasp. He chased him into the toilets so we followed them in. The editor had written a review on Ally's performance which stated that Spotty Dog from the Woodentops could have played Macbeth with more credibility.

We left the editor dangling from his shoelaces on the toilet door and the next issue printed an apology saying he might just have been a wee bit hasty in his criticism.

During the last week of third year three events occurred,the first being the Strike followed by the Beast's revenge which in turn was followed by the Teachers versus Pupils sports matches.

For some reason I can't even vaguely remember a spate of strikes broke out in various Glasgow schools, basically it comprised some pupils refusing to leave the playground and enter the classrooms.

All they did was stand en masse and chant "strike....strike".

Winker and myself were amongst them and our pals were watching events from the ground floor biology class.

The Headmaster was out with most of the teachers including McCrindle and they were writing down any pupils' names they could identify.

Winker and myself got lost in the crowd watching and listening as the Headmaster's pleas and actions were becoming less patient and more animated. The Headie eventually gave up, locked the school doors and phoned the police who came in fleets of vans at high speed across the playing fields.

As they approached those fast enough to escape got off their mark but they did manage to make a few arrests. During the melee we climbed through the window into the class and Mr Smith rather than make a big issue out of it just said sarcastically "nice of you to join us".

But......while McCrindle was out in the playground playing Herr Kommandant The Beast had gone into his classroom, nailed McCrindle's belts to his desk, sawn the legs off his chair and written, "Your'e a big sadistic bastard " on his blackboard with an aerosol.

He also just for good measure signed his handiwork T.B rules.

This led to every pupil with those initials being questioned and threatened by McCrindle who was determined to extract a confession from someone be they innocent or guilty. The Beast was never even suspected as his real initials were E.B.

While the interrogations were going on after normal school hours The Beast also let the tyres down on McCrindle's car.

McCrindle went ballistic and the next day he belted (with a new belt of course) anyone who was seen striking the previous day.

He punished each pupil as though they he was culprit who had worked him over. The pupils union was abolished the day after it started. The education department had brought in their version of the army in the form of General George Patton McCrindle.

McCrindle never did find out who was guilty but from then on he regarded every pupil as though they'd done it and treated them accordingly.

CHAPTER NINE

THAT summer we had a heatwave and we'd go down to the park to watch the girls sunbathe trying to get as close to them as we inconspicuously could without being accused of peeping.

We were into girls in a big way and by this time we'd each had a girlfriend and knew the basics of the female form which for a long time had been a bit of a mystery.

Now we knew that females enjoyed a winch just as much as we did.

It had taken a lot of trial and error to discover this. We thought they fought us off because they hated it. Now we knew it was because they didn't want to get a reputation or get pregnant.

Getting off with someone was done in a ritual manner which had to be observed at all times.

We would position ourselves in easy view then hang around like a bunch of James Deans, the girls would walk past about ten times and be ignored for the first five. By the sixth we'd make inane comments which they wouldn't acknowledge until the eighth, the acknowledgement generally came in the form of "what are you looking at, ye want a picture?" By the tenth we were conversing quite freely and only then could the courtship commence.

When I say courtship it was more like walking around the streets until it got dark enough to persuade them to go round the back of the close for a winch and a fumble.

After which your mates would ask unsubtly 'did you feel her'.

I got to know more females than my mates because I was dead sneaky, whenever anyone passed who was remotely attractive I would approach them with the ploy 'my pal fancies you'. They would ask who and I would point out Wilco sitting there in his N.H.S.glasses and plukes visible at fifty paces. They would look at me as though I was mad and say, "Him, he's a goofball".

Wilco was oblivious to the fact I was using him to break the ice and he thought I'd amazing bottle when it came to the fairer sex.

On Wilco's glasses, he claimed that they weren't N.H.S. jobs but John Lennon specials to which Ally answered, "Well he must be a prick as well then".

Now that I'd made contact with the girls I would subliminally sell myself to them and about 50% of the time it worked.

The nights seemed endless and the days just rolled into one another, we had no school and no worries, in fact the only weed in the garden was lack of cash.

On a Saturday we'd all jump on a bus and go into the city to wander round the shops, record shops and boutiques (there's a word from the past). We could neither afford records or clothes and all we could do was crowd into a wee booth in the record shop and listen to the latest releases or try on clothes way beyond our price range which was zero anyway.

Our weekly soujourns were a welcome diversion. We didn't mind weekdays because we'd have been at school anyway but shouldn't we do something even more special on a Saturday than simple window shopping.

The money problem was overcome when we went out and found ourselves jobs as paper boys and milk boys. With a bit of cash we decided we'd have enough to go to a disco in the city centre once a month.

Not that we knew much about Discos but we wanted to find out.

You see we believed what we'd seen on the telly and thought that every nightclub was like the ones Simon Templar the Saint went to.

There would be lots of girls in yellow plastic mini skirts dancing on tables and everyone would be kissing each other.

So with cash in pocket four shiny faced kids set off for the bright lights on the number 41 bus.

We got off the bus at the old Buchanan Street bus station and made for the first pub which caught our eye - The Tri- anon in Sauchiehall Street. The first obstacle was the bouncers but they were both involved chatting up a couple of girls, just glanced in our direction and nodded us in.

This pub was unlike the only other pub I'd visited and was lively, loud and full of people who looked roughly our own age.

Ally went away and got three lagers and a coke. The coke was for me as I remembered my first alcohol experiment and didn't want a repeat performance.

Ally said we should position ourselves next to the ladies toilets as sooner or later every girl in the place would have to go wee wee, that way we could check out the talent without wandering about bumping into people and looking like desperados.

No one even looked at us and disappointed we left as last orders were called at a quarter to ten.

The only disco we knew of was Clouds which was situated above the old Greens Playhouse. We got to the door and casually sauntered in.

We'd got about three feet when a large neanderthal stepped into our path.

"Whit age are ye?"

"18"

"Any I.D."

"Any idea of what?"

"Look yeez arenae 18, gaun beat it".

Crestfallen we went outside. Ally was all for going back in to challenge the bouncers to a square go. Winker just said "aye sure".

We were approached by this bloke who must have been in his 20's.

"Cannae get in eh".

Ally informed him what happened.

"The big fat bastard stopped us".

The guy went on to give us his advice.

"Aye well yeez shouldnae go in mob handed cos the bouncers don't like too many single guys in ye know. Look, whit yeez dae is go roon the corner, swop yer jaikets and get a haud of a couple of bints and ask to go in with them,that confuses the bastards to end".

"What's a bint?"

"Tsk, you know burds, touche, gimp, fanny, know".

We'd nothing to loose so we went round the corner and swopped jackets.

Once done we pleaded with any passing girls to get us in and Ally and Wilco had success first and strolled in by the bouncers with a girls on their arms.

"Christ sake it works, mon, here's two coming noo".

Two girls were heading our way from about 40 yards down the street.

They looked quite small from so far away but with each step towards us they got taller. Once alongside us they were both about a foot taller than Winker and myself. They both looked like a couple of whores in distress but what did we know.

"Hey missus, gonnie get us into Clouds?"

"Who you fuckin' calling missus?"

"Sorry can you get us in?"

"Whit age are youse?"

"18".

"Ma arse, does yer mammy know yer oot, how long have been aff the tit".

Her pal silent until now took pity on us.

"Aw fur fucks sake Isa, gie the wee boys a chance".

Isa looked at us.

"Aye fuck awright, whit the fuck, but if yeez get papped don't blame us".

So they took our arms and we headed back round the corner, I caught sight of our foursome in a shop window and the scene looked ridiculous. The arrangment looked hopeless and on entering the bouncer put his arm out and stopped us.

"Aye fuckin' right".

We thought out chances were zero but Isa came to our rescue.

"C'mon Erchie ye were young yersel wance, gie the boys a chance".

But Erchie still said no.

"Come tae fuck, the place is full of fuckin' under fuckin' agers anyway, so what the fuck difference is another two gonnie fuckin' make".

I'll say one thing for Isa, she had a certain je ne sais quoi about her.

The bouncer dithered a bit, then looked straight at us.

"Aye all right. Just this wance but any bother and I'll toe yer arses on the way oot".

We thanked him profusely, paid the entrance fee and got in the lift to take us the five floors up to the club. On the journey Isa told us, "Right we got yeez in but don't start pestering us up here awright, we don't want any of oor pals tae think we hing about wae afterbirth, awright".

Once in the club we hunted down Ally and Wilco and found them standing self consciously at the bottom of the stairs leading to the dance floor.

"Yeez got in then," said Ally very half heartedly whose confidence and sparkle had disappeared.

"What's up wae you?"

"We've been standing here watching everybody go down to the dance floor".

"So".

"Well the place is hoaching wae posing bastards wae all the best gear and haircuts. I mean fucking look at us. I've got a suit on that doesnae fit me, Joe 90 here is fucked before he starts and youse two look as though ye use Oxfam as yer Fifty Bob Tailor, we'll never get burds in here, we've nae chance".

Wilco then said something he must have read on the back of a matchbox, "Faint heart never won fair lady".

Ally looked at him as though he was going to belt him ,"Fuck up"

Winker was a bit more constructive.

"Well Ally ye can stand here if you want but I didnae pay one and a half quid to hang around the bottom of the stairs, Christ I can dae that at the bottom of the close for nothing". He beckoned to me "come on".

I looked at Ally and Wilco, shrugged my shoulders and followed Winker into the club. The music was deafening and one minute the floor was totally illuminated and the next it was pitch black, disco lights apparently.

The dancers were grouped in the middle of the dance floor and we stood at the side watching. Those not dancing were wandering aimlessly in a circle round the dance floor.

"How come everyone's walking round and round?" I asked Winker.

We soon found out when a bouncer appeared at our side.

"If you're no dancing boys ye'll need to keep moving." He then ushered us to join the circle.

After about ten laps we decided it was time for a dance.

We spied two girls dancing alone. Winker headed towards them, stopped for a second and shouted in my ear above the din. "Right we'll start with a couple of howlers and work our way up".

I followed him and tapped the girl on the shoulder. She turned, didn't even acknowledge my presence and started dancing facing me.

Winker's choice did the same.

We'd have been as well not being there as they both gave the best impressions of someone dancing alone when they have a partner than I have ever seen.

The record seemed to go on forever and neither Winker or myself could think of a lead line to break the ice, the record finished after what seemed like an eternity and the two of us left the dance floor at high speed.

"No exactly friendly up here are they," said Winker.

I could offer no explanation so I just nodded and said nothing.

He went on, "At least at the school dances we're popular, maybe Ally's right, we are out of our depth up here".

Right on cue Ally appeared with Wilco in tow. He was excited.

"Wait till you see this, it's fucking brilliant, mon".

He led us up the stairs and up to the balcony. Clouds had a balcony right round the dancefloor which was full of intimate alcoves.

He led us round and each alcove housed a couple giving it mad winching.

"So what", said Winker.

"Naw, roon here a bit, just look but for fucks sake don't stop, just keep going"

We reached the alcove that Ally was talking about and found a couple actually engaged in the sex act. We hurried by at a snail's pace and out of earshot of the couple Ally asked the obvious question.

"Did you fucking see that, fucking hell".

"Aye, mon lets go back round again".

We made four more passes and on the fifth they'd finished and were sitting smoking cigarettes.

The show was over.

"Christ sakes" said Winker, "Lets go down stairs and find some mad shaggers".

As luck would have it the Alcove Don Juan must have acquired the only rampant nymphomaniac in the place, but we did leave the disco a lot older and a lot wiser than we were two hours previously.

We walked down to George Square to catch the one o' clock late bus home. It was our first apres midnight visit to the square and we were astonished at some of the sights.

Drunks lay everywhere, people were fighting and yelling gang slogans and swearing at each other and car loads of posers were driving around and asking girls if they'd like a lift home.

The atmosphere reeked of violence and intimidation.

We joined the bus queue and tried hard not to catch anyone's eye as we wanted to remain as anonymous as possible.

The thud of the music was still throbbing in my head. All the way home I could feel it and when my head hit the pillow it kept me awake long enough to reflect on the night's events.

I had visited my first grown up disco, I had seen my first sex act and I had survived my first late night in George Square. I fell asleep with mixed feelings.

We returned to school that August the creme de la creme, our words not Miss Jean Brodie's. There were only 23 of us left out of the 200 or so who had commenced 1st year which of course is a very small percentage and this had advantages and disadvantages.

The pros being that the teaching was much more intense and the cons being that in times of trouble it would be extremely difficult to get lost amongst the throng.

During morning assembly the Headmaster called out a list of names of those who were to report to his office after registration and Winker and mine's were tagged on last. We hadn't had any time to get up to any mischief so we were a bit confused about why he wanted to see us.

We found out - he wanted to make us prefects and we of course declined because prefects are usually crawley bummie licks and we didn't want to be tarred with the same brush. He insisted, in fact he insisted strongly saying it would build our character and with no option we left his presence sporting our badges of office.

We entered our first class of term, Miss Goudie's history double period. She was in the middle of her 'how dare you come into my class' late speech when we flashed our badges, "School polis mam".

She then accused us of stealing them and it took quite a bit of convincing that the badges were genuine authorised issue. She was as incredulous as we were of the dubious honour accorded us.

During the break Winker outlined the plan he had been working on in History to get us the sack as prefects and out of the extra work involved. That lunchtime we put the plan into action.

One of the duties was to station ourselves at the bottom of the two sets of stairs leading up to the classrooms and direct first years to their lessons. At one stair I succeeded in sending a whole class of first years to the primary school half a mile away by telling them we were using it as a school annexe. Winker for his part sent 30 pupils to the Headmaster for misbehaving and he also gave the first year Geography class the afternoon off because the teacher was off sick.

The result was chaos.

The Headmistress from the primary school phoned to say she had found an entire class wandering her corridors, the pupils sent to the Headie were wandering about lost because they had no idea where the Headie's office was, and the Geography class had disappeared completely in the Devil's Triangle.

Winker and I were sitting in the common room on a free period when we were summoned.

We knocked on his door, he debadged us, called us a couple of morons and said ' he was giving us a week's detention.

"What's detention Sir" asked Winker.

The belt was to be phased out as much as possible this term and replacing it would be detention classes.

This meant a class laid aside for an extra hour's schooling each night as a punishment. We had been sentenced to seven.

As we left his office Winker didn't seem too bothered.

"It's only an hour, it'll be a laugh".

I looked at him, "But a whole week?"

"We'll have been pardoned by Wednesday,they'll have some poor diddy student in charge and he'll not be able to handle it".

He couldn't have been more wrong because on entering the detention class we found McCrindle positioned behind the desk.

"Typical, I wondered how long it would take you two to end up in here".

He warned us in no uncertain terms what would happen and basically told us that he'd thrash us both within an inch of our lives if we gave him any grief.

Apparently he was not one of the corporal punishment reformers.

Winker and I stared at the clock whilst he read his paper. Every so often he would look up to see if we were misbehaving before returning to his news.

That went on for the whole week, an hour's silence each night. Winker and I were the only pupils and this set the pattern for the entire term.

Being fourth years we now had a common room which was a great place to hide if your were dogging lessons. It had a telly which for some reason only ever picked up educational programmes, table tennis table but only one bat and a dart board.

Darts became a great favourite until someone stuck a dart in the school captain's bum and the armoury was removed.

Winker would pull the valves out of the telly and throw them four floors to the ground to hear them going off with a bang.

We had less classes now as we had all picked the subjects we wanted to specialise in and concentrated on those subjects.

But to sit the O'grades the prelims had to be passed first.

That year the school board had introduced a grading system, for instance,

A pass = 85% and over.

B pass = 75% and over.

C pass = 50% and over.

D pass = 40% and over.

E pass = 30% and over.

There was a catch however. Although you'd have to be a complete dunce to fail to get any sort of pass you could only sit the O' grade if you achieved 50% or over in the prelims.

We settled down to our studies and I still couldn't understand bloody algebra, maybe it's dead simple when you get the gist of it, you know the wee tricks but it was and still is totally beyond me.

In all our classes we had a few fifth year repeating the subjects they had failed the O grade in, of course there was no shame in this, except in Arithmetic.

Failing in Arithmetic was the same as contracting leprosy and we had two resident lepers.Our teacher in this subject was a small but muscular Malaysian man who we refered to as Precious McKenzie the Commonwealth weightlifter whom he bore more than a passing resemblance to.

Arithmetic is basic common sense, 2 plus 2 equals 4, but our two lepers couldn't quite comprehend this diffucult equation. Every time they were asked a question in class the room would fall silent to hear their comedy gem of an answer.

Leper one was a guy called Grant and although the hippy era had drawn to a close he hadn't noticed.It was rumoured that L.S.D. was responsible for his dull wit and intelligence. His one redeeming aspect was that he was a brilliant artist and the reason he was still at school was to gain enough passes to get into art school.

From what I've seen since leaving school and what now passes for art Grant should have been able to get in with a metal work O level, that and an ability to talk a load of bollocks.

Leper Two was Thuggie Millar whose name was actually Shuggie but he had a world class lisp, he could have lisped for Scotland. Thuggie's ambition was to go to Sandhurst for Officer training. Yes he had overdosed on Commando comics.

Precious I think felt sorry for Thuggie and indeed there was a lot to feel sorry for as he had the lot. Short hair, thick neck, thick lips,unlevel ears and his eyes were looking permanently in different directions, the latter being disconcerting when he was talking to you.

Precious would spend a lot of time on Thuggie just trying to make him understand.

"If I have one apple in this hand and I take it away, how many apples would I have?"

Nine out of ten times he got it wrong.

There was no higher arithmetic as it only went as far as O'grade and was classed as an easy subject, as yet no one in the school had failed it twice but these two were sure candidates.

In fourth year we now had to visit the Careers Officer in order for him to advise us and give us help to reach our dreams.

Of course we were still at the age of wanting to be pop stars and footballers with the girls coming a close second in the fantasy stakes as Air Hostesses.

The Careers officer was an intolerant man who was always throwing pupils out of his office and telling them to return when they'd grown up.

"Bloody pop star, indeed".

Winker on his visit told him that he'd like to be a career officer, he'd meant it as a joke but the C.O. took him seriously and all through fourth year bombarded him with leaflets and application forms.

I told the C.O. that I would like to be a dentist. It was the first thing that sprang to mind as I had just visited one that morning and he had a gorgeous receptionist.

He took one look at my reports and told me to set my aim a bit lower, well a lot lower actually and waved me out of his office after handing me a wad of pamphlets on employment in Cowglen Saving Bank.

The pamphlets featured pictures of happy faces seated at desks with big broad smiles and articles on the Cowglen Tennis Club, the Cowglen Badminton Club,The Cowglen Highland Dancing Club and the prospects within the Civil Service for the dedicated civil servant.

"YES YOU - can have a glowing career in banking".

The pamphlets ended up in the bin.

In October we had the "egg incident' which led to me and Winker being expelled.

We were in Nutty's science class for the last double period of the week and Nutty had to leave the room for five minutes. While he was away Winker strolled down to Nutty's desk, took an egg out of his pocket, cracked it open with a ruler and poured the contents on Nutty's textbook. Winker shut the book and returned to his seat.

Everyone in the class looked at him as though he was mad.

"What did you do that for".

"Dunno".

Nutty returned to the class and told us to open our books at page fifty two. Nutty opened his book and the egg dribbled out and onto his desk.

He went mental.

"Who's responsible for this?"

There was total silence.

"I said which one of you bloody wee bastards did this?"

Ally went "Woooooooooo, you swore Sir".

"Right Dixon, out now".

He gave Ally two of the belt.

Winker wouldn't own up and no one pointed the finger.

Nutty then went round checking everyone's bags for evidence of eggs.

I opened mine and about half a ton of red ash fell out.

"Sorry Sir,red ash sir, my football boots are in the bag".

He went round the whole class and found nothing so he sent someone to get the Housemaster Mr Nesbitt.

Nesbitt came in looking weary as an awful lot of the trouble in the school came from Nutty's chemisty class.

Nutty showed him the book and said, "I'll get to the bottom of this if these swine have to stay here all weekend".

Mr Nesbitt addressed the class resignedly, "If the culprit owns up now it will save everyone a lot of time and trouble".

No ones eyes moved and we all sat and stared straight ahead. We all thought that the whole class being punished was worth it just to see Nutty's rampant indignation.

Mr Nesbitt had a plan and as it happened it was a very very good plan.

He took all the pupils along to the common room and interviewed us one by one in his office next door.

My turn came.

"Did you see anything?"

"No sir".

"Is that all you have to say?"

"Yes sir".

He knew that the most dominant members of the class wouldn't talk but there were others who did.

He could have got the information at any point but he interviewed every class member anyway to allay suspicion.

After it was all over Winker and myself were to stay behind.

The other pupils left for home and none of them could look us in the eye except Ally who said,

"Aw well, there you go eh".

We stood looking out of the window.

"I wonder who grassed ye Wink?"

"Fuck knows".

I had no idea why I was there, after all I hadn't actually done anything.

Nutty came in with Nesbitt. Nutty was all for giving us a thrashing but Nesbitt just said matter of factly that we were both expelled.

"Both expelled "said Winker "he didn't do it, I did"

Nutty growled that I was his accomplice.

"Aye right enough sir, it was him who laid the egg".

The humour and injustice of that statement was lost on Nutty.

Nesbitt beckoned us into his office and handed us notes to give to our parents to explain why we were being booted out of school.

"Look sir it was a joke" I thought for one horrible minute he was going to say yolk. It would have been on his mind but on this occasion he declined to be humorous.

"We didn't mean any harm".

"That's as maybe Watson but it's too late for apologies".

"So what happens now sir?"

He explained that we were to pay for the book, make handwritten sorrys to Nutty and return with our parents who would then be informed of our behaviour.

I was innocent so I started to protest.

"But sir I didn't do anything".

"Yes but there are varying degrees of guilt, Watson is your pal and you didn't try to stop him did you?"

There was no answer to such logic.

Return on Monday with your parents.

As we left his office Winker apologised.

"Fucking sorry about this wee man".

The weekend was spent trying to explain my innocence to my parents who recieved my denials with the usual disbelief, my father said that there was no smoke without fire, now he was also accusing me of arson.

My parents were never the type to run up to the school to complain that somebody had belted their wee boy. I suppose they were parents of that era. Nowadays teachers always seem to be having charges of assault laid against them by parents of wee angels.

No, mine were of the attitude that If I was belted it was for a good reason. They were right. Seems today's kids can do no wrong.

Monday morning came and we appeared in front of the Headie with our Mums and Dads. You'd have thought we were at the Old Bailey and the judge was wearing a black cap the way our parents sucked up to the Headmaster.

The Headmaster for his part said that we obviously came from good homes and we were an embarrassment to our families.

I just sat there thinking that I had done fuck all.

The book had to be paid for which it was and after we had written and delivered our apologies to Nutty the matter would be closed.

So school honour satisfied the parents left and Winker and I trotted off to Nutty's class with our hastily scribbled notes.

We knocked on his class room door and entered.

He had a class full of first years who were sitting in the usual frightened silence. Nutty looked at us with extreme distaste.

We handed over our notes which he read and threw straight into the bin.

"If I had my way I would have had both of you taken outside and shot".

Winker piped up "Not legal any more sir".

"What?" growled Nutty.

"Murder sir, not legal anymore".

"Get out," he shouted.

As we were leaving I whispered under my breath, "Wanker".

Nutty shot out of his desk and came after me and grabbed me by the hair.

"What did you just say?"

"Winker sir, that's Watsons nickname".

He opened the door and shoved us both out into the corridor.

"You pair of thugs, I promise you that if I ever catch you at anything ever again I'll skin you alive and Nesbitt won't stop me".

He went back into his room and slammed the door.

As we walked back along the corridor Winker spoke, "I thought that went quite well".

Around 1973 Gang warfare was at its very worst and the Police seldom ventured into the scheme unless it was totally necessary.

Easterhouse has a reputation which spread throughout Britain and beyond.

Everyone had an opinion on how to deal with the problem, from the birch to using the culprits for cruel medical experiments .

Frankie Vaughn made a well publicised visit. He called for a weapons armistice, his angle was that as a boy in Liverpool he had encountered the gang mentality too.

There he was in no mans land with umpteen film crews following him around.

But the end of the appeal all he had was a skip full of sticks, one or two bottles and a couple of butter knives, hardly the cache he had been anticipating.

The Warfare continued.

What eventually did stop the battles, violence and territorial claims was the building of the M8 motorway which cut the scheme in half.

This kept the factions apart and only the occassional minor skirmish then occurred.

The Pak, West Rebels,Torran Toi and the Skinheads all paled into insignificance and the area settled down to relative calm.

It was quite funny but once they had lost their stature they got quite sad and pathetic. They would knock up some female gang member, get married yet still hung around the streets drinking cheap wine and reliving the old days through an alcoholic stupor.

None of them could find jobs because they were pack animals and couldn't think as individuals. Lack of brain cells and the inability to string a coherent sentence together didn't help either.

If by some lucky chance they did find employment it was usually in some menial position which required safety wear and not much else.

You have to bear in mind this was in the days of full employment.

The older we got the less intimidated we became.

On one occassion myself and Kenny were loading up the band's equipment into a Van and Kenny's lunatic Beagle was sniffing around our heels.

Suddenly the dog picked up a scent and took off like a two bob rocket in the direction of Torran road. This was the road which since our early years was basically an 'abandon all hope ye who enter here' area. Those who ventured in never returned. It was said that they ended up being eaten.

Kenny slammed the Van door shut and ran after the dog. He ran straight into Torran Toi country and half way up Torran Road we saw them - The Torran Toi. They looked at us meanly and had no idea that we were running after the dog. There were twenty of them and two of us.

Kenny screamed after the canine, "Right!!! c'mere you".

The Torran Toi looked at us quizzically then ran away!

We got hold of the dog and ran back along the way we had come.

The Torran Toi had lived on propaganda and fear but in reality were just a bunch of tubes.

We weren't after them, maybe they thought we were armed with an intercontinental ballistic missile or we were just too crazy to deal with. Who knows, but after that we had no fear of trespassing on their turf. They weren't that mad mental rules after all.

As a footnote, the Beagle Nicky was just too mad to keep in the house as among other things he ate the telephone, all the plastic out of the fridge and smashed the glass on the door leading to the verandah.

One day I visited Kenny and there was no dog. Kenny told me that his parents had sent it up north somewhere to become a gun dog.

That's what they told him anyway, I think they'd actually taken it to the Vets for the Big Sleep.

We sat our prelims in December and eagerly awaited the results as it was the first time that we had learned they would have any direct bearing on our futures.

The exams were conducted in a room with the desks placed a few feet apart out of whisper range, an adjudicator roamed up and down the aisles to watch for cheating. We were given an hour and half to complete each exam and I was confident that I would pass everything except maths.

During Maths I sat and scratched my head while Spig in the adjacent desk scribbled away like a demon, I thought to myself ,"what a bastard".

I had written my name on the paper and little else. The rest was totally beyond me......y plus x equals what. Beats me.

After about half an hour I thought that I'd better write something on the exam paper so without any rhyme or reason I started writing answers which probably bore no relation to the question. I lived in hope.

On Arithmetic I sailed through and was supremely confident that I'd passed, I finished the paper with half an hour to go and spent the remainder of the time sniggering at the facial expressions of the two arithmetic lepers who looked as lost as ever.

Me, I was good at this, so good I hadn't even put my workings down on the paper, afterall it was supposed to be mental arithmetic.

The results were due in January after the Xmas break so we'd have a good Xmas and worry about the outcome in the New Year.

The school dances were looming and due to lack of peoples in 4th, 5th and 6th year we would have to amalgamate for the purpose of filling the hall.

We were to play the gig accompanied by a mobile disco worked by Tiger Tim Stevens. Tim had risen to fame after a stint as a contestant on the telly game show Sky's The Limit.

Tim lived across the back from me and we'd played football many times prior to his telly debut but he had never cracked a light about it to any of us. When the news broke that he'd been on the box and had his 15 minutes of fame he was the butt of a million inane jokes.

Of course he didn't help his street cred by getting posters printed with the words "star of Sky's The Limit" on them!

The band had gone through a few changes by this time since we played our previous school dance glory gig.

Ronnie had left after contracting some brain virus or another and had to spend six months in the Southern General, Ally had become bored and told us to stick our drums up our arses as he'd found a burd. Kenny's father had forbidden him with the warning that 'damn banjos, tarts and education don't mix". As Kenny's father was really scary I'd have heeded his warning too.

Romance if you could indeed get it was a funny thing, full of holding hands, making plans for the future and being in love, or at least thinking you were.

The first really romantic couple in our year was Lizzie Bisset and Gordon "Gags" Thomson who became known as the Puke Twins.

God, they made everyone sick eating each other's faces in the common room, the goo goo eyes they made at each other in the classrooms and the writing of each other's names on their school bags in big enormous letters covered by a love heart.

Ally viewed the spectacle with more distaste than the rest of us.

"He's a fucking big poof", said Ally.

Winker didn't agree with this, "Well how come he's got a burd then?"

Ally explained "That's just a front int it, I mean look at his fuckin' hair, he fuckin' tongs it and in my book that makes him a fuckin' poof".

Winker was still confused "I don't get it".

"Look" Ally went on "the first thing poofs dae is to get themselves a burd to allay suspicion, fuck, everyone knows that".

We were still a bit lost.

"Well whit about the guys who've got burds and arenae poofs then"

"Look don't confuse the fucking issue, I'm telling ye the guy's a poof, have ye seen him in the shower after P.E., he's always first in and last oot, he's a fucking knob watcher".

Winker wouldn't believe it. "You're only jealous cos he's going out with Lizzie Bissett and you're no"

"Aye right, I widnae have her in a Lucky Bag".

About a week later we found out that Lizzie was pregnant. This refuelled the discussion.

"So fucking what, " said Ally " I could get a burd up the duff if I wanted tae, he's still a big poof".

Gags was a big guy and when he heard that Ally was slinging aspersions in his direction he beat him up.

All Ally would say after his humiliating doing was that he couldn't fight him properly cos he was too busy protecting his arse in case Gags tried to shag him.

He wasn't believed.

During the winter break I attended my first non smarty party, that is to say that there was drink there, real drink and not some poison that Ally provided. I didn't imbibe as I still remembered too well what had happened on the previous occassion.

Everyone else however ended up blitzed or in the very least a bit more tipsy. We played Postman's knock and Spin the Bottle, games designed to help the shy amongst us forget our inane patter and cut to the winching.

I ended up in an embrace with Slack Alice, this name was not based on observations of her sexual exploits but because she had a loose brace on her front teeth. Everytime we kissed my filling touched her metal brace and I almost shot through the roof in pain.

As usual there were those who had drunk too much and the smell of vomit became so over powering that I had to go out on the Veranda every so often to get some fresh air.

I took on an air of superiority "Well you shouldn't really have drunk so much, you were bound to be sick weren't you".

And "You know you shouldn't really have to drink to enjoy yourself"

Ally after one bout with his head down the pan looked up at me sitting next to him on the bath and said "You'd better fuck up". His head then went back into the pan and he barfed up what looked like most of his lower intestine.

Bullying was part of the normal school curriculum with the bigger boys bullying the smaller boys, the smaller boys bullying the tiny boys and the tiny boys bullying insects and small woodland creatures.

It was all done on a descending scale and as I fell into the category of the smaller boys I was bullied by a couple of fat blokes called Tanya and Porkie. These two would waddle about the school looking like Oliver Hardy and Oliver Hardy and neither had any bone in their body that any rational person could reason with.

They would pick on people incessantly which was merely just malice but one day they must have eaten some brain food as they came up with this idea of turning bullying into a profit.

This wasn't their first profitable operation though. Their previous at primary was to get a hold of your head and rub their fingertips into your scalp until you coughed up your dinner money.

It was painful and the pre runner for the hairdressers shiatzu massage they all seem to give you now before a haircut.

This time however their venture was much more cunning.

Tanya's sister worked in a biscuit factory and one day Tanya and Porkie brought into the school a large bag of broken biscuits which they offered around.

We had our suspicions and thought that they might be laced with rat poison or whatever but one pupil who was trying to curry favour with them ate one to please them. He never suffered any ill effects so we delved in.

Our suspicions were indeed justified for about a week later they came into the school demanding money for the biscuits we'd eaten.

Anyone not paying up found themselves on the receiving end of a doing.

Most paid up but Winker, Ally and myself refused despite the threats.We figured if we stayed together it would be three against two which weren't great odds but they were better than giving them money we didn't actually have.

This plan worked fine until I had a physics class with them and Winker and Ally were elsewhere. They approached me in the class before the teacher arrived in the room and demanded their money.

Because the clasroom was full of girls my mouth and my brain didn't confer and I said to them, "Fuck off ya pair of fat bastards".

Tanya hit me across the face with a metre stick and I went down beside a fire bucket. Porkie reached into the bucket and scooped up a handful of sand and threw it in my face which was by now covered in blood.

By the time the teacher came in I was dabbing the blood and sand off my face with a hankie. Not being a grass I told the teacher I had fallen into the bucket. I was well pissed off but would have to wait for back up to seek revenge.

I didn't wait long. The next day Winker, Ally and myself hid in a recess on the second floor corridor and waited till Tanya and Porkie had passed heading towards the stairs. We sneaked after them and when they both had one foot in the air to descend to the first step we rushed forward and pushed them both headlong down the stairs.

As they tumbled down with pencils, books and biscuits flying everywhere we made our escape unseen.

Tanya got his ankle broken and Porkie unluckily escaped with bruises. Justice had been served.

They couldn't prove who'd done it but had their suspicions and very much left us alone after that.

In January we returned for the new term and to our prelim results.

I passed every subject except Maths and Arithmetic. Failing in Maths was a foregone conclusion but failing in Arithmetic certainly wasn't.

Precious gave me the bad news in his class that I had acheived only 30% as he handed me the paper. I looked at it and all the answers were correct so I was puzzled and demanded to know why I hadn't gotten full marks.

"Because you never showed how you worked the answers out".

I went into indignant mode.

"What do you mean I didn't work the answers out, I did, I worked them out in my fuckin' head".

He gave me two weeks detention for swearing but I still wouldn't let it go. He was yelling at me to sit and I was yelling that I wouldn't until he reconsidered the mark.

"This isn't fair sir, the answers are right, what the fuck does it matter how I got them".

He gave me another week.

In all I got two months detention before he backed down and gave me a pass. To him it had got past the stage of being worth the bother.

I had gained a pass but lost my freedom.

In Maths I had gained a spectacular 7% and therefore would not be sitting my Maths O'level. Tranny said he was disappointed in me and said that algebra was like riding a bike, once you had figured out the basics the rest was easy.

I looked up from glancing indifferently over my paper.

"They say the same about shagging sir".

Tranny being deaf didn't hear me but the class did and went into laughter with Tranny joining in oblivious to what he was laughing at.

That January we were invited to go on a day's ski-ing trip to Glenshee as guests of Knightswood Academy. Mr Menzies had a friend who taught there and I think his friend invited us to do his bit for the socially deprived.

We were to meet at the school at six o'clock on the Sunday morning as the coach was picking us up first and then off to Knightswood which is much nearer the Highlands than we were.

We were all excited and in high spirits but totally unprepared for the weather which lay ahead.We were all in dufflecoats or denim jackets with about ten jerseys on underneath, the luckier ones also had woollen tammies and gloves.

Menzies addressed us as we approached Knightswood.

"Right, you are guests of Knightswood School and we shall behave as such. I want no foul language, no threatening behaviour and no drinking. Remember you are ambassadors for your school and I want you to act accordingly. The Knightswood pupils may speak slightly differently from you but that's no reason to beat them up".

Big Ally spoke up, "You fuckin' sure sir".

"Yes Dickson, fuckin' positive".

We pulled in at the Academy and we were all taking up the whole back section of the bus and had no intention of letting anyone encroach on our turf.

The other lot got on in full ski-ing gear. They had the lot, suits, salopettes, jackets, gloves and packed lunches.

Winker leaned over to me, "This lot must be loaded".

A couple of braver ones came up to the back, noticed that Ally and Winker were occupying two seats each and asked very politely. "Excuse me, is anyone sitting there"

"Aye oor fuckin' feet, now piss off".

They looked a bit dejected and one bent down to whisper in Ally's ear.

Ally moved his feet and let the guy sit down, "You tae Winker, get yer feet aff the seat and let the boy park it".

I was puzzled until I heard the whoosh of a can opening, these two pupils had sneaked a carry out on and were sharing it with Wink and Ally.

"We didn't want to drink at the front in case Teach caught us".

Ally, said, "Aye we cannae have Teach!!! fucking catching us can we".

Ally's tone was laced with sarcasm but the guy never twigged.

The journey to Glenshee took about four and a half hours during which we tried to get to know our new companions. There were a couple of crackers amongst them and Winker and myself moved in. We shuffled up the bus and got to where they were sitting.

Winker introduced us but they just eyed us distastefully. Winker not to be deterred said to one of them, "Nice anorak doll".

"It's not an anorak, it's a ski jacket," she said nastily.

Winker realising that he was bombing aimed a parting shot, "Tell me, do you take the hand doll"

"What!!!".

"I'm just asking ye if there's a chance of a feel behind a snow dune".

They started calling for some guy named Kevin. Kevin duly appeared and he was a school captain type, all teeth and hairspray.

"Are these two annoying you Hazel?"

"Yes Kevin they are being very rude".

Kevin then said the wrong thing.

"Why don't you go back and mix with your own kind".

Winker head butted him and his nose exploded covering Hazel in blood and snotters. Winker satisfied that this was the Easterhouse version of a witty Noel Coward type comeback left and went back to his seat to await Menzies who wasn't long in charging up the bus in a blue funk.

"Watson, what's your problem boy, don't you ever listen, that boy's nose is broken"

"Well sir maybe when they reset it, it'll no be as fuckin' far in the air".

Menzies explained that Kevin wanted to press charges for assault, now this was new to us, we never knew you could get the police to fight your battles for you. Menzie's mate came up and was about to join in the verbal barrage when Winker explained, "Sir, we were just having a laugh and he told us to get back to our own kind, sir the guy's a snob sir.

Menzies mate looked at Winker "He told you what"

Menzies mate took off back up the bus and started shouting at Kevin.

He accused him of being a snob and his remarks were only fir for the gutter. Seemed Menzies mate was a socialist.

After Kev's nose and the ice was broken things got much better. It turned out that Kev wasn't exactly popular amongst 'his own kind' and all through the day Winker was congratulated on his hard forehead.

We arrived at Glenshee and the conditions were perfect but the bus could only take us half way up the road to where the ski slope was and we had to disembark and walk the remainder.

As the Westwood pupils climbed off all you could hear were, "For fuck sakes" - "Jee-sus Christ's" and "Bloody hells" as the wind bit through our clothing.

We had never known cold like it before. Someone asked how far would we have to walk.

"About a mile and a half".

"How come sir, the snow here is up tae oor arses, can we not ski here?"

Menzies explained that this was not a ski run plus the place we were to collect our skis was much nearer the top, so miserable as hell we began the trek up the mountain. Every so often we'd hear swearing as someone fell down a snow covered hole.

We reached the top and we were issued with our ski boots, skis and sticks,the Knightswood pupils had been there before and knew the drill and had all the basics. We were a fankle of wood and metal.

We started on the nursery slopes while the real skiers buggered off for higher ground. Our instructor a German bloke named Hans ordered us to form a line in front of him.

We were skidding about all over the place and occasionally someone would go about four yards past him before falling over.

"Dig your sticks in ya".

We'd never met a German before and all we knew of his race was that we'd beaten them in the War and that they always went "Urgh" when they were shot in the Commando Comics.

He asked us if any of us had ski-ed before.

This question was met with a "Aye so we fuckin' have".

He then said Ski-ing was easy and commenced to teach us. Because Hans was suntanned and handsome the girls in the group were very attentive but we 'the lads' just wanted to have a shot.

"Come on Hans can we not just try it eh".

Hans humoured us, "You are the smartarses ya, then please if you try".

Ally went first with a "nae bother boys watch this" as he shot off down the slope. He was also shouting, 'look at me mammy I'm dancing, when he realised that he was heading straight towards a fence.

"Achtung fencen,achtung fencen'. He hit it and flew over it landing head first in a flurry of snow, wood and dufflecoat.

Hans ski-ed down to see if Ally was alright and got there as Ally was raising himself up. He shook the snow out of his hood and walked back up towards us with his skis over his shoulders.

"Fuckin' dawdle".

Hans looked at him.

"Now we learn how to stop ya".

After about half an hour he let us have our first go down the nursery slope. I looked around for Ally but couldn't see him lined up with the rest of us. I then noticed him about fifty yards away on top of this dangerously steep hill.

Hans saw him too and was shouting, "Nien nien, you are off piste".

Ally was shouting back "Naw naw, yer' awright, I've only had a couple of cans" and with that he pushed his sticks into the snow and he was off. He skied like a pro and had gone about 100 yards down the hill when it became apparent to everyone except Ally that he was heading straight into the car park. When he did notice it was far too late for him to do anything about it, he shot into the car park missing a parked car by a few inches before colliding slam bang centre into a mini bus. He stopped dead and his tammie flew off his head and over the bus. We threw off our skis and ran down the slope to see if he was alright. When we got there he was unhurt and in an arguement with the mini bus driver. "What dae ye think yer daeing parking a bus on a ski slope ya prick?"

I picked up his tammie while Hans had him by the hood of his duffle and was dragging him back up the hill.

"We see your teacher now ya".

Ally was screaming abuse at him, "Aw aye and whit dae ye dae fur an encore, invade fuckin' Poland?"

As the day wore on we forgot the cold and started to enjoy ourselves. We even became sort of proficient and joined our hosts on their slope. There isn't much to ski-ing, you go down and walk back up, come to think of it, ski-ing is boring.

Winker seemed to be falling over more than everyone else and I noticed that he always fell beside Hazel. Knocking her over then falling over himself is probably a more accurate description of events.

He would then apologise profusely, help her to her feet and give her a bit of patter at the same time. I saw she was starting to laugh at his comments and was, as they say, 'right in there'.

Eventually weary we trooped back down the hill and onto the bus for the journey home. The pupils were now evenly distributed on the bus thanks to all the new forged friendships. Winker had Hazel sleeping on his lap, he signalled me to come over and when I got there he asked me, "Any idea how I can get my zip down without waking her up".

By the time we reached Easterhouse we were alone after dropping off our guests and saying our goodbyes. It was around midnight by this time and we were exhausted. Menzies stayed on the bus and he was being dropped off in the city centre. As he was pulling the bus door shut to head off he said to Ally.

"Dickson, my office 9.15 to fill in an insurance form to pay for the dent in the mini bus".

As the bus left we could see he was laughing. Was he kidding. It turned out he was.

Studying for O'levels was a bind and as the schoolday was long enough we resented having to also do homework and would come up with elaborate excuses why we hadn't.

"Sir the dog ate it".

"Sir my wee brother ate it".

"Sir I ate it".

and

"Sir an eagle swooped down a stole my school bag".

The thing was though, most of us ended up doing our homework in detention classes just to pass the time.

The 'O' levels were important but the most important thing in my life was football.

I played for the school team, the Boys Brigade team and Celtic Boys Club.

Luckily though the school games were always played at the crack of dawn, the B.B. matches around eleven and the Celtic matches at three, so I managed to play three games each Saturday.

On the B.B.- we had only joined to play football as we heard that the B.B. teams were awful and we could look good while gubbing the opposition. In the team were Winker, Ally, Wille Burns(he of battery fame) and myself, there were others of course but they were genuine B.B. and had the badges and the Thunderbirds outfit to prove it.

We even reached the final of the East of Glasgow Cup, not that this made us brilliant, oh no, it was because the oppostion was awful.

So awful in fact that most of our qualifying matches had ended in double figures.

In March that year our English teacher Mr Smart decided for reasons unknown to field a debating team and nominated Winker, Ally, a girl in the class called Sandra, and myself as members.

None of us knew what a debating team was and in the common room we discussed it.

Ally reckoned he knew more than most. "Aye well ye see it's like an argument sort of a thing, ye get a topic and ye argue about it".

"Is that it then, we're in a team of arguers".

"Aye".

We were up against Allen Glenn's, a posh fee paying school where unless you were on a bursary your parents would be out at least a grand a term.

The first round took place at our school and the Glenners turned up in a brand new mini bus with about ten supporters and a couple of teachers doubling as judges who were supposedly neutral.

Our support comprised one teacher and the jannie who was there to lock up once it was over.

Desks were lined up facing each other and we sat looking scruffy opposite a shiny team in school blazers and nice haircuts.

The subject was Adolf Hitler - Lunatic or Genius. We drew the short straw and had to defend him.

Ally being our captain had to start us off. He got up and said, "Adolf Hitler was a genius," and sat back down again.

The judges were a bit taken aback having expected at least a few minutes of rambling. They faffed a bit until they found the bit of paper with the Glenners captains name on it and announced the floor was his.

He patted down his hair, got up, cleared his throat and began.

"How can my learned friend in the opposition state that the aforementioned despot was a genius, Adolf Hitler was a pathetic mentally deranged evil scourge of humanity...."

Ally broke in, "Naw he wisnae and he wisnae a desktop either".

One of the judges banged his gavel on the desk causing Winker who was in the process of nodding off to jump.

"Mr Dickson you have had your say and you are not allowed to interrupt the opening address".

The Glenner continued.

"Hitler destroyed, Hitler murdered......etc etc ....etc".

He went on for a full 15 minutes.

My turn came and I thought I had better make an effort of some description.

"Adolf Hitler made the trains run on time and that's not easy".

Winker whispered to me, "That was Mussolini ya tube".

"Was it, em well okay, let me see, Hitler's army had great uniforms, he made rousing speeches and he put that siren thing on the noses of stukas to scare the crap out of people he was dive bombing. I mean he beat Poland in three weeks and how many folk have done that".

As I sat down I could see Mr Smart sitting with his head in his hands.

The Glenners then went on in great depth why Hitler was a nutter. They had the whys, wherefores and hows and we sat not really understanding what they were talking about.

The only person in our team who spoke with any authority on the subject was Sandra who talked about the upsurge of the German ecomony in the 30's. When she sat down I said to her, "where did you learn all that?" and she told me that Mr Smart had been coaching her.

Needless to say we didn't win the first round and Mr Smart declined the rematch which gave them a by into the next round.

That was the end of the debating team.

Various clubs sprang up in fifth year, not exactly clubs, more like two or three pupils having their hobby funded by the council.

There was a canoeing club, a hillwalking club, a cinema club and a chess club. The chess club didn't last very long as Winker took great delight in throwing the chess pieces out of the fifth storey window.

We all joined something except Ally who was too busy running a book on what he called 'The Biggest Tits in the School contest'.

The contenders were Anne Dawson and Lesley Paterson. Ally was trying to persuade one of their fellow female classmates to nick their bras when they were in P.E. for him to measure them so he could have a winner. He didn't have much luck and it was only years later at a class reunion that we found out that Anne Dawson was the clear winner, well she claimed she was anyway. I tried to claim my winnings off Ally but he refused to pay up saying that it was unofficial.

Our first choice was Hillwalking because it sounded easy. After all how difficult can putting one foot in front of the other in a forward motion be.

One Sunday morning the club found itself at the base of the hills behind Largs. Menzies was in charge and including him there was eight of us. Menzies was dressed like Sherpa Tensing and he spoke with great authority on the basics of hillwalking, ie - map reading and survival but I couldn't help noticing that all his equipment including his map and compass were brand spanking new.

We set off up the hill but the class Fat Boy kept lagging behind and every so often we had to stop and wait for him to catch up.

This annoyed Winker tremendously "Can you no walk any faster ya fat prick".

Fat Boy was too exhausted to answer him back.

We'd gone about five miles in two hours when Menzies stopped, consulted his map and said, "There should be a crashed plane here".

No plane wreckage was apparent and Menzies looked confused so he started checking his bearings, first he'd look at the map, then at the mist covered sun, then at his compass and back to the map again.

Winker was lying on his back pulling out shafts of grass and eating them. "We lost sir?"

"No we are not lost and stop eating the grass, sheep might have urinated on it".

Winker added "Can you actually read a map sir?, I think you've been watching too many movies sir".

Menzies glared at him. Winker got up and started walking away from the party. "Watson, where are you going?"

Winker without turning round said, "For a pee, I may be gone some time".

We waited for Winker to return before setting off in a different direction and had been walking for a further two hours when he shouted

"Aw fur fuck sake, that's the rock I pished behind, we're going round in fucking circles".

Menzies grabbed him, "Don't be stupid Watson".

"Me stoopit, I'm no the one with the map".

Menzies warned Winker what he was going to do to him back at school but Winker just laughed.

"School sir, I'd be surprised if you could find it".

We broke for lunch and Winker nodded furtively for me to join him.

"You know whats gonnie happen don't ye, " he whispered, "we're gonnie end up stuck up here all night, run out of food and have to eat Fat Boy like they did in that plane crash in the Andes."

I thought this over and only ate half my packed lunch. The rest I was keeping for later.

"But Wink, how lost can ye be in Largs?"

"That prick Menzies could get lost in Safeways."

Winker was in no mood to spend the night in the hills. "Mr Menzies, what happens when it gets dark?"

"Watson it's only half past one in the afternoon and we are not lost we are simply off course slightly."

As darkness fell a few hours later Menzies admitted defeat. He told us to stay put as he was going for help. We started to collect firewood and as there was no other paper to get it going we lit the map.

Winker's attitude changed from pessimistic to philosophical.

"Aye well whit's fur ye will not go by ye....I'll bet he's planned this so he can sneak off furra bit of sheep shagging".

"Do you think people actually do that?"

"Dunno, but these country folk have strange ways."

The thing was though that we seemed to be in the middle of nowhere and had neither seen sheep or country folk with strange ways all day.

It began to get bitterly cold and as hunger started setting in Winker eyed up Fat Boy, looked pensive for a moment then stated, "Na".

The other members of the group weren't coping too well and were looking a bit teary eyed, especially the two females.

I tried to allay their fears "Look it'll be allright, maybe we should snuggle up to each other for warmth, ye know all that body heat stuff."

They decided against it and snuggled up to each other but it was worth a try though.

"What's the time Winker?", said Fat Boy.

"How the fuck wid ah know, anyway it's your fault."

"How?"

"Just fucking is, right."

Winker was just trying to amuse himself.

One of the girls suggested we have a sing song round the dying small fire but Winker was having none of it.

"Right that's it I'm offski, I'm no' sitting here listening to these bampots sing 'Michael rowed the boat ashore.'

I didn't think him leaving was a very good idea. "You'd better wait here, what if you get lost."

"Whit dae ye mean lost, mair lost than we already are, how the fuck would that be possible, we don't know where we fucking are so how the fuck can we get mair fucking lost ya wank, and anyway Marco fucking Polo had probably fell doon a fucking hole."

One of the girl's delicate ears was not used to such language.

"Do you really have to swear so much."

Winker looked at her, "Shuttit."

"Look Wink all I'm saying is that we'd better stay here and wait."

"You lot can stay here and freeze if you want to but I'm off, yeez can come or yeez can stay."

We had a quick discussion and decided to go, so our intrepid team set off into the blackness. Winker looked up to the sky.

"Right one of they starry bastards up there is the north star."

We all looked up not exactly sure what we were looking for.

"Which one."

"Probably, the shiniest one".

"That ones quite shiny."

"Okay" said Wink, "that one there, now Largs is on the west coast so if we keeping heading that way we'll hit civilisation, well...Largs anyway".

It seemed logical so we set off in the direction we thought was west.

Fat Boy was once again lagging behind.

"Are you gonnie keep up?"

"I cannae help it."

"Well let me put it to you this way, either you keep up or ye'll lag behind and the sheep shaggers will get ye."

After this warning his step had quickened considerably.

We trudged on and on and on and were losing faith in Winker's northern star theory when we heard the sound of a fog horn directly in front of us.

"See" said Winker "that's a fucking fog horn so we are going the right way. I'm a genius".

We climbed one last hill and there was Largs below us in all its splendour.

It took a further 45 minutes to reach the town and when we got there the clock on the church tower said 10.30.

We walked on until we found a police station and entered to report our predicament.

Menzies hadn't shown up so it was presumed he was still wandering about on the hills. Little could be done until first light according to the cops, so they phoned the

Easterhouse police station in order for them to tell our parents we were safe and we were put up for the night in the Inverclyde Recreation centre.

We were exhausted and with little thought of Menzies plight we crashed out almost immediately.

Around 11 the next morning Menzies was located and when they brought him down he was a babbling frozen moron. Winker couldn't resist a dig as he sat there shivering with a blanket covering his shoulders.

"Hope you were on double time sir."

Menzies was too cold to answer him.

Two other teachers arrived by car and one drove the mini bus back to the school.

With each retelling of our adventure Winker would add bits on, but when he added on a story about how we fought off a weird hill tribe who wore blue war paint the story lost a lot of credibility and so did Winker.

Our last Xmas at the school approached and we had the usual rituals of the school dance and the Xmas service in front of us. There was the usual enthusiasm for the dance and usual lack of it for the service.

It was another 4th,5th and 6th year deal due to lack of pupils and all that stood between us and the dance was the pre-lims for the highers.

This was the big semi final. We did the exams amd met after each subject in the common room to discuss answers.

No one seemed to have arrived at any of the same conclusions.

Winker tried to alleviate everyone's disappointment explaining

"Look it's down to the markers' interpretation in't it. Okay we might all have different sorts of answers but in a round about way and with a bit of the old lateral thinking they're probably roughly nearly a' a bit the same".

I figured that not everyone could be wrong, and I hoped I wasn't amongst those who were.

As there was no point in worrying until January I put the exams out of my mind.

For this dance we were allowed to choose our own entertainment and after a vote it was everyone against five in favour of a disco.

The five who wanted a band were.....the school band.

It was obvious we had our critics but Winker was philosophical about the whole thing, "Ach well if they think we're shite, that's their problem".

Being fifthies we now had our pick of the 4th year talentio and we had our eyes on a couple of crackers. Winker reckoned that to pull these two would take a bit of dutch courage in the shape of a bottle of El Dorado.

Winker drank the full bottle and I had a capfull as I was still very wary of falling face down in my own vomit and wanting to die.

The dance started at eight o'clock and Winker began tanking the bottle at 6.30 so by the time we got to the dance he had puke all down the front of his new Ber Sherman Texan shirt.

We went in and Winker draped himself over a chair. Menzies noticed him swaying while holding onto the back of it.

"Are you drunk Watson?"

Winker looked up but was too ill to speak and I had to make his excuses for him.

"No sir he's got food poisoning," then I added the immortal statement I was to hear many times in adult life, "he's eaten a bad pie sir."

Menzies greeted this with scorn.

"Oh yes, well how come he smells of drink then?"

"Ah well sir you see his maw puts Sherry in the steak pie."

Menzies went on and I could see Winker gathering his strength, Menzies declared! "I have never heard of a sherry steak pie, sherry trifle maybe".

Winker took a deep breath "Look Minger, why don't you just piss off."

We found ourselves outside via the fire exit in about three seconds flat and we stood in the cold air suitably confused by the quickness of our impromptu change of venue.

I spoke first.

"Aw great Winker, we'd only been in ten minutes ya bastard and we never even got a sniff of the fourthies."

The words fourthies had no sooner left my lips than we heard violent retching coming from round the corner. I wandered round with Winker hanging onto my shoulder and to our surprise we found our targets for the night on their hands and knees puking all over the ground.

One of them was crying, "Oh God, Oh God" and the other was whimpering pathetically. Winker seemed to be sobering up quickly thanks to the cold air and the sight of the two fourthies.

"I'd recognise those two arses anywhere, there is a God, come on."

We wandered up to them.

"Are youse allright there girls."

Neither of them was capable of speech and our presence didn't really register for a few seconds. They retched violently one more time then rifted a few times indicating that their stomachs were now free of toxins.

My favourite looked at me, "Gonnie take me hame please."

I helped her to her feet and wiped her mouth with the lapel of her jacket, "Look ye cannae go home in that state, I'll need to walk you about for a while until you get sober."

"I'm no drunk, I'm no".

"Aye sure, whatever you say, mon".

Winker meantime saw his chance and whispered to me.

"I've got the key to my Da's lock up, I'm taking this one here in there until she's compis mental enough for a winch."

We were a couple of chancers and took full opportunity of the situation and headed off in different directions.

As mine sobered up we got into a nice conversation and I decided that I liked her and would not take advantage of her being a bit on the steaming side.

Winker had no such morals but he still didn't manage to lose his virginity because he couldn't go to the lock-up as there was a gang hanging around outside it drinking cheap wine.

He had to put his love on hold until the next time.

In January we got our results and settled down to studying for the highers a few months hence. As this was our last chance we did as much as we could to ensure a pass even though occasionally we tried a way round studying.

Macbeth was part of the Higher English paper and rather than waste months trying to work out Shakespeare's dialogue we decided to go and see Roman Polanski's film version at the G.F.T. (The Glasgow Film Theatre). Hopefully that way we'd take a bit more in.

We headed into town for the early Saturday evening performance. There were four of us, Winker, Ally, Wilk and myself.

We walked in and the manager stopped us, I suppose we didn't look like the normal G.F.T. punters, generally speaking only psuedo intellectual vegetarian type people in folk singer style garb go to the G.F.T. to see sub titled so called art films and analyse the movie afterwards in the cinema bar.

"Oh yes Crawford, the darkened images definitely for me portrayed man's inner fight with the recesses of his captured pre pubescent memories".

For the want of a better phrase, they all talk pish.

We didn't fit that description and the manager said to us that Monty Python's Holy Grail was actually on at the A.B.C. in Sauchiehall Street.

"We know Mister, we're into see Macbeth".

He let us in and stood behind us with his arms crossed for most of the movie checking that we behaved ourselves.

When the exams did come there were those who were convinced they'd pass, those who were convinced that they would not and those who would take them as they came. I fell into the last category.

The first exam was Geography and although I had paid attention in class and studied all the work notes I was still reading my jotter on the way into the exam room.

I left my books on the desk specially laid out for pupils' belongings and walked to my designated desk with my name on it.

The desks had been laid out in such a way as to keep the unruly element apart.

The Adjudicator told us to turn over our papers and commence.

I scratched my head, huffed, leaned on my elbows and wished the two hours were over. Winker I could see was having trouble, was making 'fur fucks sake faces" at me but as he was too far away there was nothing I could do to help him.

The only pupil within whispering distance was Colin Smith who was a right Mr Swotty and he would on no account aid and abet with a bit of cheating.

Winker it appeared was sunk. He stuck his hand up.

"Sir I have to go to the toilet".

The Adjudicator looked at him with disgust and beckoned to his assistant to take Winker to the toilet and stay with him.

On Winker's return he sat down and attacked the paper with great gusto. He almost had smoke coming from his pencil. After the exam was over he told me he'd stashed his jotter in a poly bag in the cistern, went in locked the door behind him and had a quick bit of revision.

The Assistant Adjudicator never suspected a thing and his toilet visit was a relief in more ways than one.

The drudgery of the two weeks of exams passed leaving us free for the rest of the term to amuse ourselves as best we could.

The Common room became more of a social room where we spent our time listening to music and scanning the jobs vacant in the papers.

Once a week Ally would sneak a bottle of wine in and he'd share it with those who wanted.

The school had provided paper, stamps and envelopes for pupils to write off for jobs and luckily at that time Easterhouse had been broken up into segments with areas named Easthall, Blairtummock and Lochend. This helped because as soon as certain prospective employers saw the name Easterhhouse on an application form the applicant was at a disadvantage.

For those planning a career in the civil service, i.e. Cowglen Savings Bank the results would be very important, the higher the pass the higher the wages. Those with good grades could become clerical officers and those who hadn't been as successful would be working under them as clerical assistants.

Wilco wanted a job in Cowglen, Ally didn't care where he worked as long as he got lots of dosh for very little work and Winker and I would simply take the first job offered us.

We became more friendly with some of the teachers now that the war was over. In fact it turned out that some of them were only a few years older than us and they began telling us stories of what they got up to at school.

Winker was unimpressed with this however and accused them of belting us for things they'd done themselves.

In the common room Winker took to making paper aeroplanes out of the pages of his school books and flying them out of the window.

This ended abruptly when the janitor appeared in the common room threatening to stick them up Winker's arse.

It got a bit boring however and we got fed up killing time waiting for the last day. When it came I felt quite numb and found that I could now do exactly as I wanted, a strange feeling. I'd heard that people institutionalised for long periods always return to the only life they know back in prison or mental hospital. After 12 long years could I adjust to life on the outside?

The friends who had left in 3rd year had seldom been seen despite promises of keeping in touch and remaining pals for life.

Most of them now were nearing the end of their apprenticeships or training and were real working men and women.

I was worried that as soon as I left I'd become a hermit as everyone drifted apart.

For the first time I felt real fear of the unknown future.

I discussed the situation with Winker as he was having one last attempt at destroying the school television.

"How is this thing still working, I've pulled out every valve and we're still getting a bastardin' picture".

"I don't know Wink...last day eh".

"Perhaps if I papped it out of the window".

"I'm saying it's the last day".

"Last day of what".

"School".

"So".

"Well that's out, into the big world, get our results, get jobs, get money"

He pulled out a wire then punched the screen and sat down defeated.

"You know I'm gonnie miss this place".

At last he seemed to have found my train of thought.

"I mean where else can you look up birds' kilts or stare at their diddies without getting a slap in the mouth".

The conversation ended there.

The girls in the common room were wrapping presents for the teachers as a thank you for the years given out of their lives.

Winker said to them, "Youse are aff yer heads, they bastards get paid to teach us"

I lept to the teachers defence.

"Aye maybe so but it's a nice gesture and anyway not all of them are bastards".

Winker softened.

"Aye Menzies was a good laugh I suppose".

The door burst open and a box appeared with Ally behind it.

It contained 12 bottles of cider he'd just stolen off a pub delivery lorry.

At least Ally had some idea of the significance of the day.

"Mon, lets have a drink to celebrate".

He handed out the bottles, some declined a drink and his answer to that was "don't be such a poof," even to the girls.

"Okay, okay, best order please, five years we've been here and are last we are offski, so here's to offski".

He raised his bottle, we raised ours.It was quite an emotional moment ruined when Ally pointed at the school captain and said, "Don't even think about taking a slug ya prick, I still hate ye".

The last day came to a close and we left the girls in good bye tears in the common room and walked through the corridor towards the main door.

As we walked we didn't converse much. We were striding along like the Jets in West Side Story with our wee chests puffed out as far as they would go. We passed the graffitti we had put on the walls, the dent in the plasterboard where Winker had bounced a first year's head, in other words our everlasting monuments.

One of the footballing adults who joined in our games once told me that your schooldays were the best days of your life.

I was thinking now that if this prophesy was true I was looking forward to a pretty miserable exsitence.

We went through the door and out into the playground heading for the gate. I was scared to look back in case I was turned into a pillar of salt. There was now a bit of hesitancy in our steps. I think we all felt as though we were stepping out of one world and into another and once a certain point was reached there would be no going back.

We passed through the gate and I mentally envisaged it clanking shut behind us and the school disappearing.

In that split second 12 years of education was over, I'd spent three quarters of my life behind desks probably at great expense to the tax payer. Would we be able to justify it?

We walked on out and into the world to give it our best shot.

THE END.